GARDEN PLANS

GARDEN PLANS

NEW DESIGNS FOR SMALL GARDENS

Judy Brooks

GEORGE PHILIP

For Fre, Tamsin and especially Jessica

Title page illustration: A mown path leading to a cottage through a grassy meadow.

British Library Cataloguing in Publication Data

Brooks, Judy
Garden plans: new designs for
small gardens.
1. Gardening 2. Gardens—Design
I. Title
712′.6 SB453

ISBN 0-540-01168-1

Designed by Derek St Romaine
Picture research by Anne-Marie Ehrlich

Published by George Philip & Son Ltd
27A Floral Street, London WC2E 9DP

Filmset by Tameside Filmsetting Ltd
Ashton-under-Lyne, Lancashire
Printed in Italy

CONTENTS

FOREWORD

Two major problems face the newcomer to gardening, and for that matter anyone in the first few years of gardening. One is the design of the plot, which includes what features to put into it; the other is to find plants suitable to the soil and position.

Moving to a house with a garden usually provides one of two quandaries – either one finds a raw plot as left by the builders, full of various kinds of debris and maybe with no topsoil; or it is the established layout of the previous occupier. Sometimes it is in between, an old design which has been allowed to deteriorate, perhaps with large trees and permanent paths.

The first quandary calls for resolution and a lot of energy, but is in some ways the easiest, because having removed the debris and somehow got the soil into reasonable condition, one has a blank canvas to fill in as desired. Rather daunting perhaps, but one is the master of one's fate!

With an existing layout, whatever its condition, it is often hard to focus beyond the beds, paths and plants that are in place, to imagine how to change them if they are not entirely to one's liking. Often there will have to be compromise; there may be virtually immovable features and perhaps large trees, which one may not want to destroy or which may well be protected by conservation orders.

Either way it is easiest to sketch ideas on paper, and here is the first place in which this book, aptly called *Garden Plans*, scores. It tells the reader just how to go about this, whatever one's standard of draughtsmanship, perhaps with the aid of photographs and the before-and-after sketches which were pioneered by the famous landscape designer Humphry Repton two centuries ago.

There are scores if not hundreds of ways in which the typical rectangular plot

A mixed border of shrubs and trees with foliage of different shapes and colours.

one is likely to acquire can be laid out as an attractive garden suited to one's needs. It is probably seldom that a specific plan or three-dimensional sketch fits exactly with an individual's wishes or preconceptions, or indeed with the dimensions of his or her new plot; but all plans should have the potential to be adapted. In this book Judy Brooks has chosen some starting points, using designs based on historical models; and her chapter on garden design in history not only explains this approach but is inspirational in itself.

Inspiration is the keynote of the eight designs which are developed in detail as examples of the infinite possibilities of laying out a smallish plot. Making the garden suit the style of house is an aspect often ignored by writers on design, but it is emphasized here in all cases.

If none of the designs exactly fits the reader's ideas for his or her own garden, they ought to stimulate the imagination into a host of permutations. Equally, if some of the individual features suggested in these plans are not to one's liking, the final sections on paving, boundaries and dividers, structures and other decorative features will suggest many alternatives.

Personally I always think that the choice of effective plants is much harder than achieving a pleasing design with attractive features, not forgetting the necessities of a garden such as a tool-shed or compost heap. The beginner simply does not have the knowledge needed to stock a garden, beyond the most obvious; the problems of different soils, acidity, shade, damp or dry conditions, let alone the qualities and ultimate sizes of plants should all be taken into account.

Realistically it is a matter of gaining such knowledge through seeing plants in gardens and in illustrated books (the latter are sometimes apt to mislead, especially in matters of scale). This is inevitably a long-term process, which can mean that in the habitual desire to have quick results mistakes are made and plants grown which one is often unwilling to throw out just because something more pleasing has been discovered; especially as years of growth may be involved in terms of size and the replacement plant will be out of kilter with others around it.

Fortunately for present-day gardeners, modern garden centres not only cater for instant results, but display a good range of plants which can be seen when at their best, in flower, fruit or leaf or whatever their attributes are. It is true that garden centres do not always have the rarest and choicest plants, but most of those I know certainly provide a worthwhile selection.

Suitable plants are of course designated in all the plans presented here; they include many general favourites but also some less well known ones. As far as selection goes, the vital part of this book is the section on *Choosing and buying plants*, which admirably sets out the criteria to apply. As the author points out, many garden shrubs have a short flowering season, spending the rest of the year with indifferent foliage and none at all in winter. The lilac is an example: glorious in its three weeks of bloom, a nonentity all the rest of the year. In the small garden, only the most lilac-addicted should find room for it. Many shrubs, however, redeem a short flowering time with attractive foliage, maybe autumn colour, fruits in season, and sometimes interesting bark and form, specially important in winter. Similar criteria can be applied to other types of plant like perennials.

What makes this book specially worthwhile is the author's quiet, level-headed approach, her appreciation of factors which some writers – and I think some garden designers too – ignore, such as the ineffectiveness of shrubs like the lilac already mentioned, the desirability of matching garden to house, the appearance of the garden in winter, and a host of other commonsense points. Judy Brooks has been through this beginner's phase herself and decided to put down her experience, doubtless acquired through making mistakes, for our benefit.

To make a garden is, or ought to be, an exciting creative act. Moreover, it is an ongoing one – unlike painting a picture or producing a piece of furniture, which remain the same when complete – because, to quote the author, 'gardens . . . evolve and change within the framework of the design'. In a quite unpretentious way, the excitement and the creativity involved in garden-making are what come through in this text. It is clear, it is thoughtful, it does not talk down, and it is full of adaptable ideas.

Anthony Huxley

INTRODUCTION

Garden styles and fashions have undergone revolutions at least as great as those in clothing, art or architecture. This is true even in the twentieth century, when the whole scale of gardening has been reduced from the grand schemes of earlier ages. Today we measure beautiful gardens not in acres but in square metres. There is still a small number of people with gardens on a scale that would be recognized by 'Capability' Brown, but there are millions more who have only a fraction of the land but who still want to make a garden that gives the same kind of pleasure. On this modern scale, 'landscape' may seem a rather large word to use, conjuring images of the wide sweeping acres of eighteenth-century Europe, but the concepts of landscaping still apply to gardens today – even small ones.

We also look at time in a different way from the gardeners of the past. Planting any garden means thinking about the future, and the great gardens of the past were laid out by men and women who had their grandchildren in mind, but most of us today live in houses that we do not expect to occupy for the rest of our lives, let alone leave to our descendants. Our twentieth-century impatience for instant results leaves little room for the peaceful anticipation of slowly maturing trees.

Labour-intensive gardening has become relatively far more expensive than it was before. Very few gardens, whatever their size, are able now to employ the army of head-gardeners, under-gardeners and gardener's boys that were commonplace before the social upheavals heralded by the First World War. More gardens today are maintained solely by their owners and, to some extent, this dictates the layout of gardens as well as the plants that are grown in them. Evergreen shrubs and paving, for instance, need much less attention than trim lawns and herbaceous borders.

There is, of course, an infinitely wider choice of plants now available than there was five hundred years ago. New varieties are bred continually and the trickle of imports, that began with the Romans and increased with the explorations of the Renaissance and the discovery of the New World, had become a flood by the nineteenth century. On the other hand, some flowers, once overwhelmingly popular, have declined; some garden plants are even thought to be in danger of extinction.

There is some fascination, though no particular virtue, in making a garden which is genuinely a historical replica, and planting only species and varieties that are contemporary with its style. But it is by no means essential. An Elizabethan rose garden must contain only those roses that Elizabethan sources indicate were grown at the time, but a rose garden planted in the same style, with carefully chosen modern varieties, can provide a very similar atmosphere and, perhaps, even greater pleasure since today's roses offer a wider choice and a much longer flowering season. Some combinations, anachronistic mixtures of plants and styles, are less successful, but our ancestors would undoubtedly have envied our varieties and hybrids.

There is now also a new conflict in gardening, between those who see a garden as a place in which to grow plants, either flowers or vegetables, and those who see the garden as an extension of the house, open to the air but subject to just the same rules of design, utility and colour co-ordination. In the last century, there were so many new plants that they became a matter for collection – the rarer the better. This has left us, perhaps, with an urge to fill the garden with as many plants as possible, only one of each kind, more or less regardless of how they look together and how they make up the garden as a whole. Then the pendulum swings and the result is a garden in which the structure is everything and the plants some kind of optional overcoat. In between lies the view that plants are what make a garden a garden rather than a recreation area. In any garden, and in small ones in particular, the strength and clarity of the design around which they are planted are what make it work. Both are important. Neither can be neglected.

The motivation behind building a particular garden has echoes throughout history; a place to walk, a place to hide from the world, or show off your horticultural skills, a complement to the house, a view, or a screen. All these are reasons behind garden-making today.

In the eighteenth century, when gardening fashions underwent one of their periodic revolutions, those who followed the fashion did so in the belief that they had in some way got it right whereas their predecessors had got it wrong. Now there is a less strict regime in horticultural style, and more freedom to innovate, but also more freedom to choose from and enjoy what has gone before.

In the Pleasaunce *by Atkinson Grimshaw; a Victorian view of the small garden.*

GARDEN DESIGN IN HISTORY

Looking at the ways in which gardens have developed over the last five hundred years or so, there are very many trends and influences which have worked changes and affected how gardens are made today. Social changes at home, as well as startling discoveries and innovations from all round the world, have played their part at different times but, inevitably, most of the gardens and sights that influenced our ancestors have long disappeared. Today, we see them only in pictures and paintings, or as archaeological remains.

It is clear that practical considerations were often at the heart of early garden design and that different cultures devised similar solutions to the same problems. For example, small beds which are accessible and easily maintained are seen in wall paintings in the tombs of ancient Egypt and in medieval paintings from many European countries; today they still make one of the best ways to organize a vegetable garden.

In the heat of North Africa, the greatest constraint on gardening was, and no doubt still is, the need for quantities of water. The dates, figs and vines depicted in the Egyptian wall paintings must have needed daily watering. To be close to a ready supply of water, most gardens were laid out along the banks of the Nile and many had irrigation channels or canals cut through the river bank, which fed fish ponds on the way, and brought water to the hearts of the gardens.

A central waterway or canal also became a major feature of garden design in other countries. It appeared in the gardens of Persia and, following the spread of Islam, in India and in Spain. The Romans built canals in the gardens round their country villas, and they were revived again in the classical gardens of the Italian Renaissance. From there they spread to France and eventually to northern Europe. The seventeenth-century French designer Le Nôtre, whose spectacular ideas were the delight of Louis XIV, conceived the cruciform canal at Versailles which measures 1.8 × 1.5km (1.1 × 1.3 miles).

The straight lines and geometrical forms created by the channels and canals that were originally designed purely as waterways are the origin of the formal garden. It was from them that the seventeenth-century French designers drew inspiration for the axial symmetry and mathematical intricacies of their gardens, to which they added stairways, statues, classical architecture and a grand scale.

On the other side of the world, there was a heritage of gardening that could hardly have been more different. The Chinese began gardening with the advantage of a very beautiful natural landscape, and this helped to shape a philosophy which was concerned with the harmony between nature and man. This is expressed in their natural approach to gardening, which contrasts with the western approach of cutting, taming and generally beating nature into submission. The Chinese have the longest uninterrupted gardening tradition in the world; Japanese gardening was probably derived from it more than a thousand years ago, when European gardening had hardly begun.

The most immediate and startling difference between this tradition and that of Europe, perceived by the first European visitors to the Far East, was the lack of symmetry in oriental gardens. Everywhere shapes were irregular, and water, stones, rocks and carefully chosen plants were used to make exquisite and often symbolic pictures. In some places, a whole garden became a craggy mountain-

An Egyptian papyrus painting (1340–1300 BC) of a prosperous family in their garden. The regular-shaped pool, fringed with a variety of palms and fruit trees, was an essential feature of such gardens. Drawings like this, part plan, part picture, often make it possible to identify precisely the trees and plants.

scape, created with informal groupings of rocks. To travellers, the contrast with their own gardens at home must have been enormous. When they returned to Europe, they took back with them a rather naive view of what oriental gardening was all about, but it had some influence on landscaping in Europe in the eighteenth century and on architecture, both inside and outside of the garden.

In Britain, around the beginning of the sixteenth century, a growing interest in gardening was marked by the publication of the first horticultural manuals and herbals. Gardens of the time were still generally walled and plants were grown in small, symmetrically arranged beds, called knots, which were divided into segments by patterns of dwarf hedging, often of box, and each was planted with a different species, or scattered with earth or gravel of different colours. Early in the century the beds were surrounded by low railings, often painted in red or some other bright colour that would be unusual in a garden today. But, as time went by, these were abandoned. The origin of these rather complex little beds is sometimes explained as being the need to make the most decorative use of a relatively small number of fairly subdued-looking flowers, which were all that were available at the time, but knots were also planted in warmer parts of Europe, where the range of plants was wider.

Beyond the knots and the courtyards, there was an increasing use of statuary and fountains; topiary was beginning to be used and mazes abounded. Some of these are thought to have been religious in origin – they provided a sufficiently long and uncomfortable route for penitents shuffling on their knees. Some early mazes were laid out in turf, with a contrasting path of gravel, rather than being embedded between dense hedges, in the way that is now thought of as traditional. Others were hedged mazes, the sort you get lost in, and were also sometimes given a Christian significance; they were compared with the arduous journey of life, with many puzzles, corners and surprises, but leading, after many trials, to the goal – the heart of the maze and the discovery of some relic or heavenly ornament.

The real excitement of garden design in the sixteenth century was centred in Italy. There it was a time for man to express his wit, his elegance, his status and, above all, his absolute mastery of nature – this was all expressed in the ways gardens were laid out. Each estate vied with the next for the grandest fountains and the most spectacular grottoes. The most famous was, perhaps, the garden of the Villa d'Este, arranged under the patronage of a competitive cardinal, the Governor of Tivoli, who was determined to outdo the efforts of a rival cleric, Cardinal Farnese. Like many gardens of that time, it was characterized by lavish and ingenious waterworks, including water-powered musical instruments and elaborate practical jokes that could soak an unwary passer-by. From Italy, the rest of Europe borrowed the use of architecture in the garden, building gazebos, temples and obelisks into garden design; they borrowed too the idea of a scale of gardening that was grander than before, and the use of water for its vital and ornamental qualities.

An eighteenth-century Mughal miniature showing a prince and his favourite consort in the garden. The garden is divided into four by a typically cruciform pattern of paths, with ponds and flower beds in between.

Fountains at the Villa d'Este at Tivoli in Italy. These gardens contain particularly fine examples of the ingenious waterworks that were popular in Europe during the seventeenth and eighteenth centuries.

In the seventeenth century, the magnificent gardens created in France during the reign of the 'Sun King', Louis XIV, set the model for gardens elsewhere in Europe. The gardens at Versailles personify the time; an age of grandeur and symmetry, with lavish detail on an enormous scale.

In Britain, these European influences became increasingly more obvious throughout the seventeenth century. Visitors to Italy were inspired by their experience to construct buildings as part of the garden. Knots were on the whole replaced by the similar but larger and more complex *parterres de broderie* seen in France. Gardens were more extensive than before, consisting of a formal framework built round the house, which extended into long straight rides that cut vistas through the surrounding woodland. It was as if orderly, rearranged nature was stretching its fingers into the wilderness of the countryside.

The introduction of new plants also had a great influence on gardens of the seventeenth century. At first it was incidental to general exploration, diplomatic contacts and the founding of colonies, but by the seventeenth century men such as the Tradescants, father and son (both called John), were planning and setting out on expeditions themselves to find new plants. Both were passionate collectors who supervised private botanical gardens. John the elder, who was also gardener to Charles I, went to the Netherlands, where there was a strong gardening tradition, and later to Russia and Spain. His son is usually reckoned to be the first plant hunter to have crossed the Atlantic and to have introduced plants from the New World.

The new plants were detailed in herbals and dealt with by nurserymen, the most famous of whom were George London and Henry Wise, who were also among the last of the formal garden designers before the great revolution in style of the next century. It is the name of George London, rather than the city, that is remembered in the name of the hybrid saxifrage, London pride.

Throughout the sixteenth and seventeenth centuries, gardening in Europe largely followed the lead of Italy and France but, as the eighteenth century approached, there was the beginning of a revolution. Various writers, including the

The parterres de broderie *in the gardens of an English country house. This highly intricate form of gardening originated in France and was the height of fashion in seventeenth-century Europe.*

diarist John Evelyn, began to question accepted garden style and to argue for the inclusion of something in a garden that imitated nature. As the century progressed, the controversy continued. William Kent was one of the first landscape designers to put the philosophy of 'natural design' into practice; as Horace Walpole wrote later that century, he 'leaped the fence and saw all nature was a garden'.

These early gardens were not as open as the landscapes that followed them, but they incorporated natural themes and views as well as statuary and an incredible range of buildings, temples and follies. A journey round the garden, a walk or a drive (depending on the size of estate) was an important part of enjoying the effect. The poet Alexander Pope was another early exponent of the style who designed a garden in Twickenham aiming to provide 'contrasts, the management of surprises and the concealment of bounds'. His 'surprises' included a shell temple, an obelisk dedicated to his mother, a small amphitheatre and a grotto.

The key to the 'concealment of bounds' and the end of the domination of walled gardens lay in the devising of a sort of submerged wall called a 'ha-ha'. This is a ditch with the vertical side nearest the house, generally faced with stone, and the other side sloping gently up towards the farmland beyond. The result was a stockproof boundary, visible from the farm side only, and given its name, apparently, from the exclamation of surprise 'Ah-ah!' with which its discovery was greeted, rather than the explosion of mirth implied by 'ha-ha' or 'haw-haw', as it is sometimes spelt.

The result of the ha-ha was that the boundary of the garden (or park, as it had become) was no longer visible. The garden no longer reflected the architecture of the house but, instead, turned outwards and was integrated into the landscape. The designer's aim was a perfect view, and to achieve this 'natural' phenomenon lakes were dug, trees were felled and farms rendered 'picturesque'. Garden designers composed a picture just as carefully as their more formal predecessors had, but they moulded the scene with a subtlety that concealed their art.

From the eighteenth century, there is one figure who is remembered above all – 'Capability' Brown. He was not by any means the only, or even the first, landscape gardener, but he became so well known for his assessment of the 'capability' or potential of a site that his nickname is known by all and his Christian name, Lancelot, often forgotten.

The landscape gardeners did not have it all their own way, however. One critic expressed the wish that he should die before 'Capability' Brown so that he could 'see heaven before you had improved it'. But the fashion for landscaping, however, prevailed to the extent that there are few earlier gardens remaining; most were levelled and changed beyond recognition, their capability fulfilled by Brown or one of his colleagues. Of many magnificent seventeenth-century gardens, all that remains are plans, paintings and shadows in the grass where the beds stood and fountains once played.

In the next hundred years there were changes in every aspect of life, and gardens were no exception. The new middle class created by the Industrial Revolution lived in modern villas with smaller gardens, and wanted a style which would display their wealth and success. There was an enormous fascination with the torrent of new plants from all over the world. Novelty was an obsession as gardeners grabbed at the discoveries of plant hunters and the hybrids of plant breeders. Intricate beds reminiscent of the seventeenth-century *parterres de broderie* were fashionable, but this time they were planted with brilliantly coloured bedding plants which had been raised in the greenhouse.

Glasshouse gardening took off on every scale, from the domestic conservatory to the glass halls of Crystal Palace. The gardens of big country houses employed hundreds of men to keep every corner of the garden at the peak of perfection throughout the year with successive bedding of greenhouse-raised plants. The result was often brash and grandiose, the style that comes to mind when 'Victorian' is used as an insult.

In the later years of the century the long conflict between formal and informal surfaced again in Britain with the work of William Robinson. He recognized the importance to a garden of a formal plan, but hated that same formality when applied to the arrangement of plants. His greatest venom was reserved for 'the absurd daubs of colour' of formal bedding, and he advocated instead softer, asymmetric borders planted with herbaceous perennials. Gertrude Jekyll, who designed many gardens, large and small, is perhaps the best known of his followers. She wrote about design, horticulture and her whole approach to gardening in a way that can still inspire.

At much the same time there was a renewed interest in gardens from the Far East, and the beginning of a fashion for Japanese gardens, but the combination of west and east was not always successful. The images of Japanese gardening – clustered rocks and mossy pools – were, and still are, used without much understanding of the philosophy behind them, and without the skill and craft of trimming and training that is needed to make the shapes characteristic of the style. Architecture and artefacts, bridges and pottery were often used without proper support from the overall design.

Through the last two or three hundred years the meaning of 'small' in a garden has changed. 'Capability' Brown designed a 'small' cottage garden of three hectares (eight acres); the new Victorian villas built in the nineteenth century had 'small' gardens of about one hectare (two or three acres). Now those same areas have been divided again to make 'small' gardens for modern houses – small, but with a long heritage to exploit and enjoy.

The romantic view of the cottage garden by the Victorian watercolourist, Helen Allingham, showing the typical straight path from the gate to the front door, with mixed beds on each side.

DESIGNING A GARDEN

Before designing your own garden, you need to sort out three quite separate sets of facts: firstly, what you already have; then what you really must have (in the way of boring domestic essentials); and then what you want from the garden, in terms of use and appearance. The temptation at this stage is to rush things, to hire a mechanical digger and plough up the entire garden or make an extravagant outing to the garden centre to buy shrubs and trees that you have no idea where to plant when you get home. Resist it.

Stages in the development of a small town garden, planned on a series of interlocking circles. Stone, granite sets and brick are used in the path and in the paved area at the end of the garden, which is made secluded by a substantial trellis.

Begin by conducting a kind of survey. Take a thorough and detailed look at what kind of garden there is already, before planning how to modify it or, indeed, bulldoze the lot and begin again. Preserve your observations by making a plan of the garden on which you can record the position of everything that is built or planted or growing there already. Start by choosing a suitable scale, and making a plan of the plot. The minimum scale that is useful is 1:100 (i.e. 1cm on the plan for every metre in the garden); in a smaller garden use 2cm or even 3cm to each metre.

To measure the garden, you will need a long tape measure, a ball of string with a skewer tied to one end, and a couple of extra skewers. If you do not have a long enough measure, then mark the string at one-metre intervals and measure lengths by counting the marks and only using a tape for the last few centimetres. To draw the plan you will need a ruler, set square and pair of compasses. Squared paper makes the job easier, but is not essential.

Begin by measuring and putting on to the plan any parts of the outline of the house and garden that are composed of reliable right angles. This alone may give you an outline of the property. If your garden is of a less regular shape, plot the position of the boundary by triangulation, which is very simple, particularly with the marked-up string used for measuring. Stick the skewer into the ground at a fixed point at one side of the house and, using the string, measure the distance between this point and one corner of the garden. Note down this length and then repeat the process using a second fixed point at the other side of the house. On the plan, set your compasses to the measurements taken, reduced to scale, and locate the corner by drawing intersecting arcs. Once you have a plan of

the outline of the garden, make several copies of it to use when trying designs later on. (You may find that there is a ground plan in the deeds of the house, which will save some drawing.)

The position of other existing features in the garden can then be found – either by measuring from that point to a right angle on the house or fence, or by triangulation – and marked on the plan.

CONSIDERING A LAYOUT

This is also the time to take a good look at the garden from every angle. Look at it from the house, especially from windows where you may spend a lot of time. The window over the kitchen sink is the obvious one but think as well about where you might sit at a desk, or the first early morning view of the garden from a bedroom. Look at how you get into the garden and think about ways of making this boundary integrate house and garden rather than separate them.

At this point it sometimes helps to make a few sketches of what you can see, not to be preserved as works of art but because actually drawing something, without the least expertise, makes you look at it carefully, so that you may spot something that you particularly like or loathe. If you really cannot face putting pen to paper, then take some photographs. Look out for features outside the garden which will be part of your view and could be enhanced if you like them or camouflaged if you do not. If you live in an area undergoing any development, it might be worth checking with the local authority to find out if any of their plans will change your view – establish an eyesore-blocking clump of trees before the offending building goes up.

The finished garden, planted with greyish foliage to complement the existing purple-leaved tree on the right. The use of containers, including square Versailles tubs, means that a fairly lush effect like this could be achieved in the first year of planting.

Outside the house, look at each side of the garden. Find a spot which gets the sun at a time of day when you might want to sit in it, and look round the garden and at the house itself from there. Observe which parts of the garden catch the sun at different times of the day, and remember too that because the angle of the sun varies by as much as 45° throughout the year, the amount of the garden encompassed by the sun will be different in winter.

Having taken on board the state of the garden as it is and the various practical essentials, it is time to think about what you want. A good way of trying various designs and effects, and getting some idea of the finished garden, is to use photographs and an overlay. Take photographs of the house and garden from a number of different angles, and have them blown up sufficiently large to be comfortable to work with. On the whole it is better to use black and white rather than colour prints, because the important thing about a design at this stage is its shape and mass. The colour of the flowers comes later. Stick an overlay made from transparent plastic on top of the photograph with masking tape and draw on it the garden as you would like to see it. (Plastic sheeting is easier to use than greaseproof or tracing paper because the marks can be wiped off.) It is an extremely simple and effective technique. Even an overlay made from greaseproof paper will enable you to get some idea of what the garden will look like when your ideas have been put into operation.

Aim to draw in the solid shapes of the garden, including the silhouette of the skyline, as well as the main areas of flower beds, shrubs, paving or lawn. At this stage the basic forms of the elements which make up the garden are more important than the species of plant, the colour of flowers or the material used for paving. It is not that these details lack importance, just that they are better decided later. It is a fascinating exercise to use the same photograph with different drawings on successive overlays, to see how changing the style of the garden can alter the whole appearance of the house.

It is important not to forget the character of the house when planning the garden, not because the house and garden need to be matched precisely in period, every Victorian house compulsorily surrounded by parterres and carpet bedding, but because they do need to be compatible in style. Starkly modern houses lend themselves to strong geometric designs rather than the cluttered informality that would best complement a thatched cottage. Many new houses need an 'anchor' – some shrubs planted close to the house, for example, which will link it visually with the ground. A frame of shrubs round a new house is also the fastest way to make it look established and lived in.

In the country, there is often scenery beyond the garden which can be used when you are composing the whole picture. In a town or suburban garden the

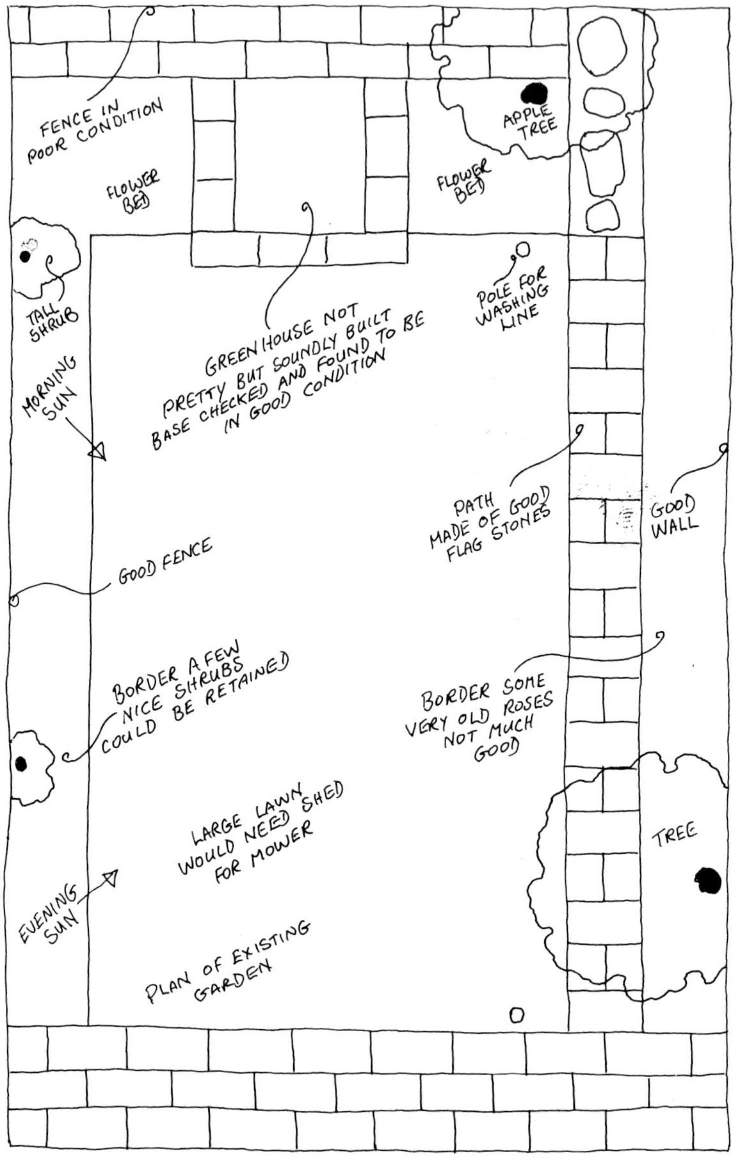

A plan of the existing garden with greenhouse, path, borders and a wide, featureless lawn.

need is often quite the opposite – to create privacy and seclusion. The ideas of wide open spaces may be attractive, but not when it is achieved at the cost of a view of every garden in the street. To create a garden which is secluded without being box-like and claustrophobic, you need to look not only at the boundary fencing (see page 166), but also at the scale of the planting.

To some extent it is true that when you have a small garden you need to concentrate your attention on small plants – certainly you have to steer clear of saplings that will grow into giant trees – but there are too many small gardens which are planted with nothing else. The height of a tree can make a garden feel sheltered and secluded. Climbers and wall shrubs will raise the effective height of a fence, making a barrier which is dense enough to provide privacy, without looking like the inside of a box. Herbaceous and mixed borders also need to look lush and bulky, and they fail in a small garden if they are scaled down too much, particularly when set against a rather bleak wooden fence.

There are some gardens which are given a very strong style by the use of one or two large-scale plants which would generally be regarded as being far too big for a small garden: plants such as *Gunnera manicata*, which comes from Brazil and will grow to 3m (10ft) or so, with vast, umbrella-like leaves, but which needs moist soil and grows best beside water; or some of the big rose species, such as *R. roxburghii*, which makes a huge clump when established, striking because of its attractive bark and leaves as well as its highly unusual green hips; or the giant climbing rose, *R. filipes* 'Kiftsgate' (this is not the kind of rose to grow flat against the side of the house, but it will scramble for 10m/33ft or so through hedges and trees or over the roof of a building, supported and kept in place by its backward-growing thorns). All these would probably be described as 'unsuitable for a small garden', and they should certainly not be planted on impulse – if only because their size excludes so many other plants – but used carefully they can be very successful.

Faced with a small garden that you want to look as spacious as possible, the immediate temptation is to put plants round the edge and leave as large a space as possible, empty, in the middle. In fact

A photograph of the garden, taken from an upstairs window, overlaid with the start of a plan for the new garden.

A mass of intermingling bright colours and tangled foliage blends with the cottage thatch (opposite)*, while the sparser, slightly Japanese style of the modern garden* (above) *similarly complements the design of the house.*

most small gardens look more extensive if there is some kind of division of space. On a large scale, different 'spaces' in a garden can be marked or separated by rather vague and unclear boundaries; distance and the eye do the rest. In a small garden the divisions need to be much clearer.

This clarity and firmness of line is one of the most important factors in almost any garden design, but is most critical when working on a small plot. If a garden is given its shape and line by plants which are deciduous, then it will lose all that in the winter when the plants lose their leaves. This means that the lines of the garden should either also exist in the structure – paths, walls, ground surfaces and so on – or they should have some kind of evergreen framework.

Making some division of space has other advantages as well. It is a good way of preventing a long narrow garden from looking like a tube. It also makes for a smooth transition between one garden style and another, and has been used in this way for centuries. By convention the part of the garden nearer the house has generally been the most formal and colourful, softening with distance in both shape and hue. This practice makes good sense in a small modern garden; the closer part is seen in greater detail, where individual plants are easily distinguished, whereas paler colours and softer lines in the distance increase the feeling of space. It also gives a chance for the style of the house to be reflected instantly in the closest part of the garden, either in shape or symmetry or in the colour of brick and paving. Using something bright and striking at the bottom of a garden tends to foreshorten it, which can, again, be a useful way of making a long narrow garden feel squarer and less tubelike.

Another temptation to resist in a small garden is that of including a large number of garden features all built or planted on a very small scale, because it generally ends up looking cluttered and bitty and even smaller than it actually is. Fewer features on a proper scale give a much better feeling of space.

The line and shape of a garden need to be balanced. In a formal garden this might mean that it is symmetrical; in other circumstances it is more likely to mean that a feature on one side of the garden is 'balanced' by another feature of roughly equal visual impact on the other. A garden with a sideways slope, which gives it an odd rather uncomfortable appearance, can be balanced by a strong mass, perhaps shrubs, on its downhill side.

In terms of balance, it is important to think of the garden not only as a map or a view, but also as a place which exists in three dimensions. For this reason it is sometimes a help to draw the garden from an upstairs window. Whether you make a drawing on clean paper or take a photograph and use an overlay, this viewpoint gives an outlook which is neither a plan nor an elevation, and makes it easier to imagine the garden in three rather than two dimensions. For anyone not accustomed to drawing and sketching fluently, this is not the easiest of perspectives to put on paper, but it repays the effort by making the final look of the garden much clearer.

Balance presents another problem when planning a garden. The way in which plant features will offset each other can be visualized only by imagining the plants when they are mature. Making this jump of imagination is very important because, when buying and planting them, the relationship between the sizes may be quite different. Particularly with shrubs, it is very easy to put them in with the smallest in front of the largest, as they are when they arrive from the nursery, forgetting that in five years' time the sizes may be reversed.

Even when planting with meticulous care, taking into account predictions of mature size, there will always be occasions when a plant grows more or less than you expected and so throws out your calculations. Perhaps this is why gardening is regarded as an art rather than a science. It is certainly part of the pleasure – gardens are not 'made' like a piece of furniture or painted like a picture, which once complete stays the same for ever; they evolve within the framework of the design that has been imposed.

When you are happy that your drawings, however clumsy they may be, have captured the shape, mood and style of garden that you want to create, transfer these ideas on to the outline plan. It is sometimes argued that this plan is not necessary; gardens are made in the soil, not on the drawing board. Undoubtedly

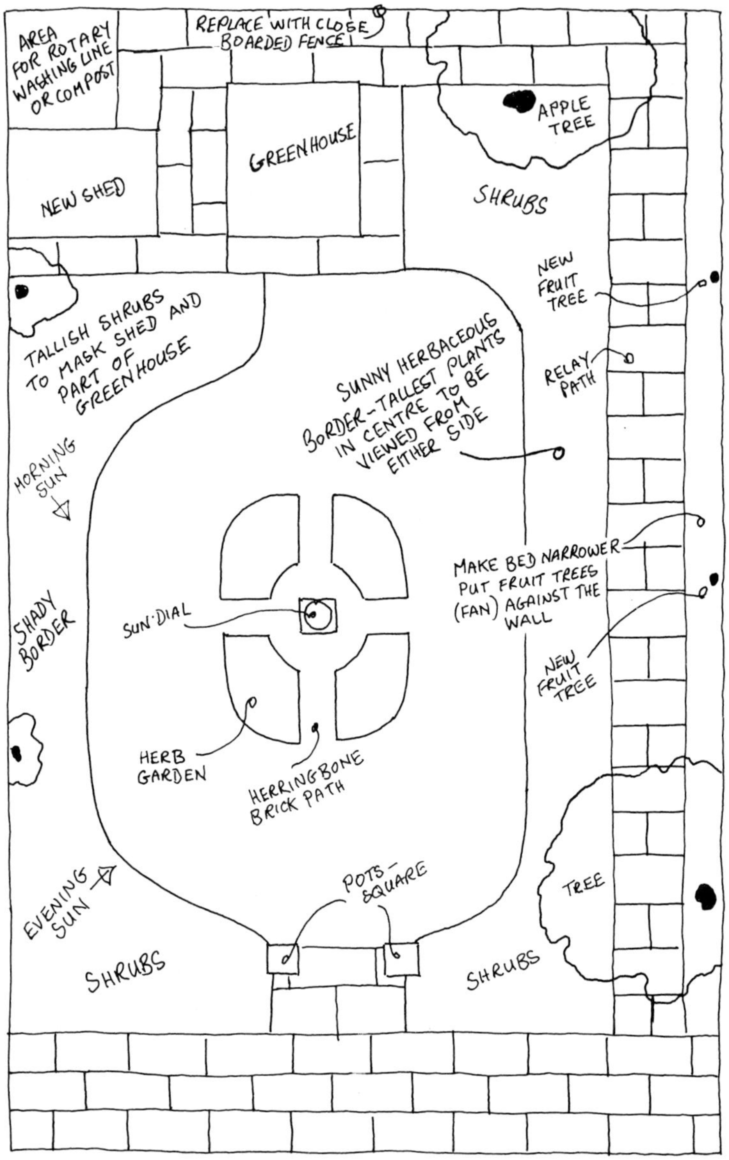

Right: *A photograph of the existing garden from ground level, overlaid with a drawing of the new design as it might look when planted. The washing-line which dominates the right-hand side of the lawn has been replaced by a rotary drier, concealed by the shrub border and shed.*

Left: *The new plan. The path is moved closer to the wall, making a narrow bed for fan or espalier fruit trees, to take advantage of the sunny brick wall. Between the path and lawn there is a herbaceous border and on the shadier left-hand side of the garden the shrub border is extended and curved round to hide a shed – almost essential for storing tools and mower in a garden this size. In the centre of the oval lawn is a sundial and herb beds, seen from the house beyond a pair of square pots. The greenhouse is retained, but made a less dominating part of the view by surrounding shrubs.*

it is truc that very many beautiful gardens have been made without committing a premeditated design to paper, but if you are the slightest bit uncertain of how to proceed with your garden, it does provide a way of trying out ideas before you begin, formulating and comparing alternatives and then recording what you eventually choose. It is not an essential process, but one that can be very useful.

Once the outline is satisfying and complete, clothe it with detail by planning the kinds of plants, the material for paths and paved areas and all the details that make a successful garden. In a small garden, attention to detail is inevitably more important than when working on a larger scale. The choice of plants is vital, and minutiae such as corner stones and edgings are more noticeable, contributing to the impression of the whole. All these 'garden ingredients' are covered more extensively between pages 121 and 188.

Now transfer the major features of the plan back on to the garden, using the same string and skewers and compasses as before. As far as you can, actually mark out what you are going to do on the ground. Bang stakes in where there will be trees so that you can confirm that they are in just the right place, because if the trunk of a tree and another vertical, such as the fence or shed, very nearly coincide, it may irritate you for years to come. Check each element from every angle. Use lines of stones, or cut the corner from a sack and trickle silver sand to show where paths and beds will be. Scatter sand more liberally to indicate areas of lawn or paving. Even put down big cardboard boxes or build wigwams of sticks and canes where there will be shrubs. Then walk round the garden so that you can get some idea, however scant, of how it will feel when it is complete. Bear in mind that this is the kind of process from which the phrase 'back to the drawing-board' is derived, and try a number of alternatives.

PRACTICAL NEEDS

In any small garden there are a number of fixed essentials, practical needs and functions that assert themselves and must be considered. So when you begin, make a list of all the practical essentials needed by you and your family.

You may need somewhere to keep

A colourful and easily maintained informal courtyard garden, with shrubs and flowers in pots.

dustbins, which should be fairly close to the house for ease of access, but not so close that the smell might intrude in hot weather. They can be screened with a wall, hedge or trellis, or put into a kind of cupboard built of brick or timber, as part of a system of raised beds, or in a side access to the garden.

Washing lines are another problem in that they are necessary some of the time, but ugly when not in use. There are now a number of devices which enable you to stretch a line between two or more fixed hooks or supports and rewind it when not in use. These make it possible to run a temporary but secure line across part of the garden, between, perhaps, the wall of the house and a fence post. When not in use, the line disappears into an unobtrusive box. Rotary dryers stand and spin in a pipe or socket and can be lifted out and moved when the washing has dried. It is important, both for its function and appearance, that it stands vertically and continues to do so for many years of use. Although you can set one up by doing no more than hammering the socket into the ground, it is better, in the long run, to set it in a block of concrete. Install it before either paving or turfing, and make sure that the top of the pipe is just below ground level so that no one trips over it and the mower can run smoothly over the top. If you want to be able to use a washing line throughout the winter, then it is virtually essential to hang it over a paved surface.

This early stage of planning is also the time to consider a source of water or electricity at the far end of the garden. Electricity cables must be contained in protective pipes and are usually buried, so it is particularly important that this is done before the garden is laid out. Safety is most important, and cables should be installed either by or with the advice of someone qualified and competent.

Taking a source of water away from the house to provide an outlet at the bottom of a long garden can also be very helpful. This can be done with a hose pipe, either buried or run along the bottom of the fence. At the far end install a tap, perhaps with a short hose for watering nearby, or run the hose into a tank with a valve that shuts off the supply when the tank is full. This sort of system is particularly useful in a greenhouse; watering cans can be filled instantly with water at air temperature by dipping them in the tank.

You may also need a shed or tool store, particularly if you have a mower. Greenhouse, garage, fuel store, car space or conservatory; all these and others, less obvious, will need to be considered before beginning a design.

Children and their needs are commonly regarded as a problem in a small garden. Indeed, there are those who go further and say that the two are entirely incompatible. If you have children, they certainly need to be taken into account because you can be quite sure that they and their friends will both use and abuse the garden. It must be designed, as far as possible, to survive these attentions and be a pleasure to everyone.

One important consideration, especially with very young children, is their safety. For example, in a garden where there are toddlers it is not safe to have an unprotected pond. Some people compromise by putting in a sandpit, knowing that it can easily be converted to a pond later. This is not a bad idea because, relative to the life and development of a garden, children's needs and interests are transient. A great deal of effort can go into constructing some plaything that will be redundant in only a couple of years. A 'shelf' at the side of the sandpit can be a seat now and a support for marginal plants a few years hence. With any kind of sandpit, incorporate a cat-proof lid.

A garden designed for young children, but with an eye to the future. The sandpit could become a pond, and the arch holding the swing already supports a flowering climber.

The balance between grass and paving is also important where there are children. Grass is softer, but is easily spoilt if well used in the winter, when it is wet. Paving may crack more heads but will take bicycles right through the year. There is no formula which will produce a solution for all, just a number of possibilities to be juggled and considered.

One aspect of children's behaviour which can generally be relied upon is that, when in a hurry, they will always take the shortest distance between two points, more or less regardless of what lies in between, so bear this in mind when siting flower beds across the garden's main lines of communication. Children are not the only offenders. Where there are any functional parts of the garden which are used very regularly, it is best to site them so that they are approached by a direct path. If a path detours round an unnecessary curve, however attractive the line, the temptation to take a short cut will be almost irresistible and the lawn, or whatever becomes the trodden path, will very soon suffer.

Taking account of these practical considerations is vital. There is no sense in a garden that looks wonderful but causes irritation by making it impossible to park the car, dry the washing or feed the rabbit.

STARTING THE GARDEN

Once the plan is complete, the next question is how to begin putting it into action. In some cases, this depends on the scale of work involved. If there is considerable earth-moving to be done, for example, this must be done first. The ideal way to proceed would be changes of level, earth-moving, etc., followed by building, fencing, paving, paths, then a thorough preparation of the soil; and finally, when all is made ready for them, the plants themselves.

There are, however, any number of factors that may disrupt this scheme. One is money. Different materials may cost more or less, but almost any paving, building or fencing will be fairly expensive. And, although shrubs and trees may, over the years, give such pleasure that they are a bargain by any standards, they too can be a big outlay if you need to fill a garden all at once.

Another factor is time. If you plan to lay paths or a patio, dig a pond or construct a trellis yourself, then you need plenty of time in which to do it. What is more, you need free time at the season of the year that is best for the job in hand. It is very often not possible to plan a garden and then just go ahead and carry it out – you need a system of priorities.

The important thing is to retain your plan, so that however long it may take the garden to evolve, all the work you do can be directed towards achieving it. The first priority must be any work that would badly disturb the garden if it were done later, and this includes such operations as level changes and fencing. After that, you have rather more flexibility. For example, once an area to be paved is clearly marked out on the ground in the garden, actually laying the slabs becomes a less urgent task. So, if the alternatives are paving this year and buying the trees and shrubs next year or vice versa, then it might be better to choose the trees now so that in a year's time the garden has new paving and trees which are well established, rather than the other way round. Providing you have not actually planned something entirely outside your scope, the order can be adjusted to fit the circumstances.

Whether you are working slowly towards a design or not, it is well worth keeping a record book of the garden and its progress. It is very easy to forget exactly which plants have been put where, particularly with something like bulbs which are out of sight for much of the year. There are printed gardeners' record books available, but there is really no need for anything so formal. You could just as well use a scrapbook, in which you stick seed packets and any labels which are attached to trees and shrubs, with their names and details of cultivation or pruning. You then have a reminder of precisely which species and varieties you buy and how to care for them. Keep note too of brand names, colours and specifications of any equipment, slabs, bricks, etc. so that they can be matched and replaced if necessary. These are the kinds of details that seem unforgettably vivid at the time, but fade beyond recall in a few months or years. If, in addition to these vital facts, you are someone who enjoys writing – and later reading – a diary, a garden is the perfect subject.

Think now also about how much time you want to devote to your garden and how much gardening you will enjoy. There seems to be a prevailing belief that the only time well spent in the garden is time spent doing nothing. All the odds and ends of jobs about the place are labelled 'work' and therefore to be avoided if possible, an attitude which takes no account of the infinite pleasure to be had from pottering in the garden, doing the small, not very arduous, chores that make a garden look well loved. One of the pleasures of a small garden is the ease with which you can acquire an intimate knowledge of the health, growth and personality of every plant.

THE GARDEN PLANS

The garden designs that follow exploit and adapt some of the themes and ideas that have been used in gardens of the past. For each one there is an illustration showing how the established garden would look, a ground plan to help in using the design, and other, smaller drawings to explain some elements of the garden and its construction in greater detail. In many cases alternative plants are included, so that these designs need not be followed strictly but can be adapted to suit different tastes.

THE COTTAGE GARDEN

This garden is designed for a rectangular plot. In front of the house is an area of brick laid in a herringbone or basketweave pattern, with small plants, including herbs, growing in the crevices. Beyond the paving is a circular lawn, also edged with brick and surrounded by beds planted with an informal and characteristically colourful mix of annuals and herbaceous perennials. A simple wooden bench is placed to one side. At the far side of the lawn is a gate leading through an arch of trained fruit trees to a small grassy orchard underplanted with spring bulbs. On each side of the gateway is a widely spaced trellis covered in vigorous, scented roses. On the brick wall at the end of the garden are several different honeysuckles, and the garden is enclosed on each side by a mixed hedge which includes flowering garden shrubs as well as several more reminiscent of a wild country hedgerow. The informal design and the use of traditional or 'old-fashioned' plant species are an important part of the feel of this garden which would work with many urban houses, not just with a typical thatched cottage.

Left: *A thatched cottage like this cries out for a traditional cottage garden, but the style can be used equally successfully with many other types of house.*

Opposite above: *An accumulation of pots, all terracotta, sit comfortably together on the herringbone bricks, in spite of their widely varying styles.*

Opposite below: *Apple trees on a dwarf stock, trained as a single tier espalier to make an edging for a brick path in a basketweave pattern; this is an unusual and effective way of growing fruit.*

If you use the phrase 'a cottage garden', in a sense everybody knows what you mean, at any rate most people have an image in their mind's eye that fits the label. It is an image of plump, rosy-cheeked children playing amicably on the doorstep of a thatched cottage. There is a mass of scented honeysuckle round the door and climbing roses cluster about the windows. On either side of the path to the door there are flowers – nothing very rare or complicated, just random patterns of all the traditional English country flowers. It is the image of a thousand Victorian paintings and countless birthday cards. On the edge of the garden there are neat rows of cabbages and perhaps a beehive. A little farther over, and certainly beyond the eye, there is the earth closet.

Historians argue about the origins of the cottage garden. Was it a sentimental Victorian myth, an insult to the penniless and exploited cottagers who were too concerned with feeding their families to worry about the hollyhocks at the garden gate? Or did the smiling ploughboy wend his way homeward in order to sow flowers in his own tiny corner of a green and pleasant land? The fact is, that whatever its true origins, the cottage garden has influenced all manner of gardening in the twentieth century and, if the sales of birthday cards can be taken as an indicator, it is an image that casts as strong a spell in the space age as at any time before.

Originally, of course, the garden round a cottage was no more 'designed' than the cottage itself. Both evolved from the needs of their occupants rather than a designer's pen and there is no famous name, no 'Capability' Brown or Le Nôtre to associate with the style. But, in spite of these vernacular roots, the tradition and style left to us by the cottagers is clear and unmistakeable.

The cottage garden as a rural tradition would certainly not lie comfortably round every house today. The symmetry and severity of much post-war housing and other urban environments would be discordant with this kind of garden but, on the other hand, a thatched cottage is not compulsory to achieve this style and many suburban houses are compatible with it.

The typical cottage garden contained flowers and fruit, herbs and vegetables all grown in close proximity. The owners of great houses might keep their pleasure gardens and their kitchen gardens strictly apart, but the cottage gardener mixed the two together, sowing flowers round the crops grown to feed the family. This mixture continues to be a part of the appeal of these gardens, even though the convention now is, generally, to separate flowers and vegetables, whatever the scale of the garden. But the element of a cottage garden that modern gardeners seek to capture is the image of a casual, colourful abundance of flowers, and the vegetables are often abandoned altogether.

This 'cottage garden' is planned for a suburban, semi-detached house, built between the First and Second World Wars, with a small square, or rectangular, plot that backs on to a brick wall – part of an adjacent building. In several ways it is quite unlike its original. There are no vegetables, although herbs and some fruits are grown here, and there is a lawn for sitting or eating.

The design is very simple, a compromise between the apparently careless unconcern of the cottage garden and the need of every small garden for a clear and firm design. Massed climbers surround the door and a riot of informal colour comes from the annuals and herbaceous perennials in the flower beds. The strong shape of the circular lawn in the centre emerges most clearly in the winter, when the herbaceous plants are dead or dormant, and this helps the garden to retain some feeling of form and purpose even when most of the plants are gone. The shape of the lawn also, incidentally, makes the flower beds rather more accessible. This is particularly useful on a clay soil, which is easily compacted by treading. A greater proportion of evergreens in the beds would give the garden more interest in winter, but this would also alter its character, because most of the typical cottage flowers are either annuals or herbaceous perennials.

The paving is of brick, with the larger or bedding face up, laid in a herringbone or basket weave pattern. Round the circular lawn is a frame of bricks laid with the narrow or stretcher face up, and with crevices between to allow for planting. There are also a few plants in crevices between the bricks. Quite a few small plants thrive in paving because the soil beneath tends to remain moist but also well drained, so that the plants have their roots in cool soil but their faces in the sun. Some of the small plants in the flower bed, such as *Limnanthes douglasii*, will overflow into the paving. This is an annual, sometimes aptly called the poached-egg flower, which often seeds itself from one year to the next. Several species of *Sedum* do well, as do the perennial *Aubrieta* in all its colours, *Arenaria montana* and *A. balearica*, creeping Jenny (*Lysimachia nummularia*) and *Veronica prostrata*, which is a kind of speedwell with bright blue flowers.

Some herbs have prostrate forms which give off a scent when trodden, such as creeping thyme and Corsican mint (although this is not very hardy). *Soleirolia soleirolii*, which also goes by the unhappy names of 'baby's tears' or 'mind your own

Left: *A series of honeysuckle-covered arches echoes one of the colours in the herbaceous borders below. The yellow flowers and foliage combine successfully with the blue, and the informal spilling over of plants on to the path softens its edges.*

Opposite: *A bed of mixed spring perennials and bulbs in front of a palisade fence. As the leaves of the bulbs die back there is space for the planting of summer annuals.*

business', has similar tiny leaves and forms a dense mat which can frame every slab in an area of paving, but sometimes becomes a nuisance if it then creeps further into the garden. There are very attractive gold- and silver-leaved varieties, but these are not as hardy as the species which, although it is often scorched by frost, always seems to come creeping back. Alpine or wild strawberries also do well between paving, and can be eaten into the bargain.

The design shown here follows the cottage convention of a central passage down the garden. The flower beds are enclosed by a trellis and from the lawn the pathway continues through a gate in a short, arched tunnel of fruit trees, into a grassed area with a few small fruit trees – a tiny orchard.

Making a tunnel by training plants over a series of arches is an idea which has been used for many centuries; it can be seen in illustrations of medieval gardens and was a way of growing vines in ancient Rome. The arches have been made from many materials in the past, but this garden uses commercially available steel supports, and can be planted with either apples or pears. The trees are cordons; that is they are pruned to grow as single stems which fruit on short lateral spurs along their length, and are tied into the arch as they grow. It is a rather exciting way of growing fruit in a small garden; there are enough trees to grow a number of different varieties, so that you can have cookers and eaters, early ripeners and good keepers all in a small space. In addition, there is the pleasure of walking through a tree-lined tunnel, even one like this which is only a couple of metres long.

The green-painted gate is made from standard 'palisade' fencing with rounded tops, but the slats are fixed to the supports so that the top of the gate forms a curve which echoes the shape of the arch above. It is not a difficult gate to make and is a good example of how to make the best of the cheap kits of fencing materials that are sold in every store, by assembling it in a way that is more interesting and original than that suggested in the instructions.

There is room in the orchard for three apple trees grown on a dwarfing stock, but the trees should be high enough to form a background to the garden. Do not choose one that will make the trees lower

than the height of the tunnel and trellis. M9 dwarfing stock normally restricts trees to rather less than 3m (9ft) in height, and this would be ideal. In very cold regions dwarf fruit trees may not be hardy. The choice of varieties is enormous and an entirely personal one, and in a garden like this with room for several different varieties, there should be no problem in selecting varieties that will cross-pollinate successfully.

The orchard is sown with grass, and underplanted with clumps of daffodil bulbs, but it is important to leave a circle of bare earth about a metre across round each tree, so that there is no competition for water or nutrients while they become established. In a few years, when their root systems have grown larger and more efficient, the fruit trees will not need this advantage and the grass can be allowed to grow up to the trunks, which will improve its appearance. The daffodils will be visible from the house in spring, before the herbaceous perennials and annuals in

Clusters of spring bulbs, naturalized in grass. Most bulbs, but especially daffodils, are much more effective when planted in groups or clumps than in regular lines.

the flower beds block the view, and the grass in the orchard can be left long so that the daffodil leaves are not damaged and can rebuild the foodstore in the bulb ready for the next year.

The way in which the daffodil bulbs are distributed when they are planted makes an enormous difference to their final effect. Straight rows look dreadful, the municipal mentality at its worst. Spreading them randomly, but evenly, is not much better, although eventually each bulb will reproduce and form enough bulblets to make a clump, which is the way that they look best. This will take some years, so the best way to arrange daffodils is to mimic their natural growth by planting them in loose, irregular clusters rather than in lines, circles or any other regular shape.

One of the best species to naturalize in grass is *Narcissus pseudonarcissus*, which is the wild daffodil found in much of Europe and so justly and famously celebrated in verse. It is a little smaller than most modern hybrids, about 30cm (12in) high, and perfectly graceful, with a lemon-yellow trumpet and paler surrounding petals. But because planting an orchard like this demands several hundred bulbs it is essential to consider the cost when choosing the species or variety. Bulb merchants sometimes offer bulbs for naturalizing in bulk, by the sack, and these can be a good buy. If you buy a mixture of varieties, plant them in separate clusters.

Once the daffodil leaves have wilted, the grass can be mown, but it should be kept at a length of about 5cm (2in) so that it is noticeably longer than the circular lawn, and the effect is one of orchard grass, and not a mown lawn with trees. One corner of this orchard is also an inconspicuous place to put a shed or compost heap but, if the length of the grass makes access difficult in early summer, only a narrow path should be mown before the daffodil leaves have wilted enough to be cut.

This orchard is also an ideal site for a

beehive – hardly an essential part of the design, but a very fitting accompaniment to a cottage garden. Kept properly, bees are not a great danger or inconvenience, even in a small garden. They enter the hive along a distinct flight path and anyone standing in the way of that may be stung, but this is the only area at risk; if the hive faces the high hedge, the bees are forced to fly over the top of it and a well-used insect pathway will be safely above head height. The fruit trees will also benefit; many fruit farmers actually hire bees to help with pollination. The honey is wonderful and bees are kept successfully in the heart of many big cities. Unlike other garden livestock they are not subject to formal planning requirements, only that they should not be a public nuisance. The straw skeps seen in cottage-garden paintings have gone; the most suitable type of hive remaining is probably the WBC, named for its deviser, W. B. Carr.

Between the flower bed and the orchard is a trellis, widely spaced, informal in structure and planted on both sides. On the flower-bed side there are climbing roses, two old Bourbon varieties – 'Gloire de Dijon' and 'Zephirine Drouhin' – both pink in colour, well scented and repeat flowering. They are vigorous plants which will grow above the hollyhocks and other tall herbaceous flowers. On the orchard side of the trellis there is a row of currant bushes, like a low hedge, with a thornless blackberry ('Oregon thornless') growing above it. This has rather pretty, fernlike foliage, some of which lasts through the winter, and good fruit, although not perhaps with quite as much flavour as some of the thorned varieties. Filling every part of the garden in this way is very much in keeping with the economics and traditions of cottage gardening. Vigorous plants, however, close together like this, demand a lot from the soil, so the ground must be very well prepared before they go in and it is important to continue to mulch and fertilize regularly afterwards.

Right: *Roses, herbaceous perennials and shrubs divide this long lawn into a series of smaller spaces, each secluded from the next. The paving stones prevent wear on the grass at the narrowest points.*

Opposite: *A painted cast-iron seat beautifully surrounded by lilies and flowering shrubs*

Brick edging to the lawn defines its shape, allows the plants to overhang without damaging the grass and makes mowing easier.

Planning the planting of the flower beds involves perhaps more restraint than anything else, because there are so many possibilities. Cottage flowers are not restricted by colour – the garden should have every hue possible. Many of the typical plants are annuals, and these could be used entirely but, in some ways, a mixture of annuals and perennials is more practical. Most garden annuals need to be planted in the spring. If you are ill, forced to go away, very busy at work or in any way at all distracted from the garden at this time, then your temporary neglect will be glaringly obvious for the rest of the year. If the garden has a foundation of perennials, there may be gaps but not quite such a disaster.

Choosing perennials and bulbs for these beds means choosing a range of heights and colours for as much of the year as possible, and a way of doing this is outlined in the grid system on page 140. This is a graphic way of recording the plants you plan to use and of ensuring that no size of plant or season of the year is ignored.

Many of the plants which can be used are recorded inhabitants of old cottage gardens. Others lack these historic credentials but would suit the context and, especially, extend the length of the season in which there are flowers in the garden. Concentrate on the softer colours of 'old-fashioned' flowers and some wild flowers; on the whole, the very brilliant, even rather harshly coloured, half-hardy annuals look their best in formal bedding and do not contribute to the atmosphere of a cottage garden. There are more details about choosing and caring for flowering plants on page 140.

The smallest of the flowering plants overflow on to the brick edging round the lawn, with the very tallest as a background against the hedge, but tall plants are also grown at the edges of the flower beds nearest the house. This gives a foreground to the view from the house, so the garden as a whole is seen through flowers, and also increases the seclusion of the lawn.

In a cottage garden the herbs are mixed in with the flowers, but planted close to the path and the house for easy picking. There is fennel, both green and bronze, and a rosemary bush among the taller plants near the house, with towering lovage, its huge yellow flower heads heavy with bees. Sage, parsley, marjoram, sorrel and lemon balm are within reach; there are a couple of buried buckets of applemint and spearmint similarly sited, and the smaller herbs, such as thyme, edge the brickwork. The annuals and those that are slightly tender – basil, coriander, French tarragon and bay – are clustered together in pots, so they can be moved into shelter, or into the house, when frosts begin. It is a good place too to give many house plants a summer break in the garden, raising some on logs or inverted pots to give variations in height and compose a balanced picture.

There is fruit in the garden, and herbs, but no rows of vegetables. There are, however, a couple of globe artichokes towards the back of the bed. These are short-lived perennials, unfortunately not very hardy, but they are worth trying, both for the pleasure of a home-grown exotic vegetable and for their striking appearance, which resembles that of a gargantuan thistle.

The end wall of the garden encloses the orchard. Growing on this wall are two species of honeysuckle: the Japanese honeysuckle, *Lonicera japonica halliana*, which is evergreen, very strong-growing with small, but beautifully scented, creamy flowers, and *L.* × *brownii* 'Fuchsoides', which is semi-evergreen with rather unusual, striking red flowers, but not quite as vigorous. Before planting strong climbers like this it is important to clean and check the wall thoroughly, and then to fix eyes and wires at intervals to support the plants. Given decent supports, these species of honeysuckle will form a dense cover over a surprisingly large area of wall. *L. japonica* will grow farthest. It flowers on the current season's growth, and these new shoots are best stimulated and thickened by shearing over it in early spring. *L.* × *brownii*, like most of the deciduous honeysuckles, flowers on older growth and needs trimming only if it gets straggly.

In the corners of the garden, between the hedge and the wall, there is on one side the shrub rose 'Nevada' and on the other a tree mallow, *Lavatera olbia*. This is a slightly tender but very fast-growing shrub which needs a warm position and well-drained soil. It has wonderful, pink, trumpet-shaped flowers, similar to the flowers of *L. trimestris* (which is an annual included in the flower beds) and an incredibly long flowering season, lasting from late spring almost until the first frosts. Although it is not hardy in cold districts, it is easily propagated from cuttings and grows so fast that cuttings taken in late summer will flower the following year.

The garden is bordered on its two sides with a mixed hedge. There are details of suitable shrubs for a hedge and how to plant and arrange them on page 166. In a cottage garden the hedge should be planted to echo a wild hedgerow with typical native shrubs such as holly, hawthorn, spindle and elder (or their garden cultivars) with a lacing of garden shrubs for extra colour. One problem with any informal hedge is that it easily becomes very wide and encroaches on the rest of the garden. This can be overcome to some extent by tying the hedge into a supporting fence. Shrub roses fit well into a cottage-garden hedge, and once it is established the hedge will also carry some climbers, such as *Clematis tangutica*, which has yellow flowers followed by fluffy seed heads, clearly related to the hedgerow 'old man's beard'.

Growing against the house are two roses, 'Madame Albert Carrière' and 'Aloha'. Both are pink, although 'Madame Albert Carrière' is rather paler and more vigorous. Both arc rcpcat flowering, but 'Aloha' will probably have a stronger second flowering. In combination, they should show flowers on the wall of the house right through the summer. The back door is framed by two deciduous and highly scented honeysuckles, the 'Early Dutch Honeysuckle' (*Lonicera periclymenum* 'Belgica'), which flowers through middle to late spring, when it is overtaken by the 'Late Dutch Honeysuckle' *L.p.* 'Serotina' which will keep flowering until autumn. On the other side of the door there is *Jasminum stephanense*, another scented climber, slightly less vigorous than the better known *J. officinalis*, and with paler leaves and pretty pink flowers. Against the shelter of a house, it is more or less evergreen and the stems curl as they seek supports, framing the view from the doorway with a little green right through the winter.

A row of mixed shrubs, trimmed to make a neat but colourful hedge around a modern garden.

THE GARDEN OF THE FIVE SENSES

This small paved garden is based on ancient Persian and Islamic gardens, which were intended to appeal to all five senses. It has fan-trained fruit trees, flowers to give colour as well as scent, the soft sound of a small fountain and different textures of flowers and leaves. Throughout the garden the paving is grey in colour but with different materials and shapes to give variation in texture. The central part is on a lower level than the perimeter beds and the pathway, and has a gravel surface with beds outlined in cobbles and grey granite. The cruciform canals of an Islamic garden are echoed in the gravel by cobbles and low-growing herbs and the plan focuses on an octagonal pond, a shape which is repeated elsewhere in the garden. The small beds around the pool are planted with different bulbs and annuals as the year progresses. The beds round the edge of the sunken garden are planted with herbs and other herbaceous plants against a hedge of roses. The garden is enclosed by a close-boarded wooden fence covered with roses, a plant that features prominently in this garden as it did in Persian gardens of the past.

The word paradise originally did not have a religious connotation, but meant simply a garden. It comes from the Old Persian word *pairidaeza*. A similar word existed in Hebrew and then in Greek, and was used by Xenophon to mean a Persian enclosed park or pleasure ground. Eventually the garden became the Garden of Eden, and then Christian writers used the word to mean 'the abode of the blessed'. It is in this sense that it first appears in English. This little excursion into etymology serves to emphasize the importance of the garden in the culture of Islam, with ideas and philosophies which have percolated into our own.

One of the ideas in gardening that spread into southern and northern Europe was that gardens should appeal to all five of the senses. They should please not only the eye but the nose, with fragrant herbs, flowers and roses; the palate, with delicious fruits; the fingers, with soft tactile leaves; and the ear, with cascades, fountains and the singing of caged birds.

The small garden, although on a scale which prohibits vast cascades, tries to do just that – but without the caged birds. There are fan-trained fruit trees to provide something edible; a mass of perennial and annual flowers to give colour as well as scent; there is the soft sound of a small fountain, and many different textures of flower and leaf to touch and enjoy.

The central part of the garden is on a lower level than the perimeter beds and pathway, and this makes an area that is both sheltered and enclosed, where there is a feeling of seclusion and still air to enhance the scent of the flowers. The

Above left: *The different textures of brick paving and cobbles add interest to a small herb garden.*

Below left: *An eighteenth-century Persian carpet designed so that the pattern follows the plan of a typical garden, divided into four parts by a cruciform canal. The geometrically shaped beds are planted with a variety of trees, shrubs and smaller flowering plants.*

Opposite: *This cross-shaped pool, with its octagonal centre, would be another suitable shape where paths or canals intersect. The low 'bubbler' fountain gives some movement to the water.*

surface of this sunken garden is gravel, with the beds outlined in cobbles and grey granite sets. In a Persian garden the paving would have been of ceramic tiles, but in colder climates this would be hopelessly impractical: the tiles would crack in frosts and be dangerously slippery every time it rained. The use of a mixture of materials and shapes keeps something of the feeling of detail and pattern that was created by tiles, without being difficult to use or too fussy in design for such a small area.

The layout of the sunken garden is symmetrical, focusing on a geometrically shaped raised pond, and this octagonal form is repeated in the other beds and shapes in the garden. Water was of enormous importance in Islamic gardens, both symbolically and practically, because most were made in hot climates. The gardens were often divided into four parts by canals which radiated from a central pool or from an ornate pavilion.

In this garden the division into four is retained, but using an ornamental channel of cobbles, interplanted with low plants. In each quadrant there is a flower bed, planted with different bulbs and annuals as the year progresses. Round the edge of the gravel is a narrow bed, planted with a low hedge of cotton lavender (*Santolina chamaecyparissus*) which has feathery grey foliage with a pungent aroma. Young plants should be set 30–45cm (1–1½ft) apart and pruned each spring to give a mound of dense, silvery growth. Left unpruned, cotton lavender will reach 60cm (2ft) in height and carry neat, yellow flowers. An alternative choice is a low-growing English lavender, such as 'Munstead Dwarf', which reaches no more than 60cm (2ft) when in flower and remains a neat 30cm (1ft) or so the rest of the year.

One step up from this is a second narrow bed, planted with herbs and other herbaceous plants, and a further step higher there is a hedge of *Rosa rugosa*. This is a native of western Asia and is, with good reason, the most popular rose for hedging. It has rather wrinkled-looking foliage, bright green in colour, and although it is not repeat flowering, it carries attractive hips in autumn. The variety 'Plena' has double flowers.

This hedge borders a paved pathway which runs right round the garden. The paving is of octagonal concrete slabs, with square granite sets used to fill the gaps left when the slabs are fitted together. There are a number of paving materials in this garden, with different textures, but all in shades of grey. Those used in bulk – gravel and paving slabs – are pale, with the darker cobbles and sets providing a contrast.

The garden is enclosed by a close-boarded wooden fence, and between this and the path there is a narrow border with a narrow, flowering cherry, *Prunus* 'Amanogawa', on each side. This tree has slightly fragrant pale pink flowers in the

Mixed climbing roses bordering a formally paved path.

spring; it does not flower before the leaves appear, but for a while the flowers generally obscure the slightly pink juvenile foliage. The most striking thing about it is its narrow, columnar shape which remains as the tree matures. In this garden it introduces some spring colour as well as the cherry blossom that is so typical of sixteenth-century Persian miniatures.

Roses were the most valued part of a Persian garden. Some of the very oldest roses would look lovely here – *Rosa gallica officinalis*, once called the apothecary's rose, has double flowers in shades of pink, whereas another variety, *R.g. versicolor*, has petals brilliantly streaked with red and white. This rose is also called *Rosa mundi* and is said to have been called after Henry II's beautiful mistress, the fair Rosamund. *Rosa damascena*, thought to have been given its name because it was introduced from Damascus, is the rose that provided the red rose which was the symbol of the house of Lancaster, while an early hybrid, *Rosa × alba semi-plena*, was the white rose of York. These are still very lovely plants, but they only flower once and they are all quite bulky, so in a small garden they have been somewhat overtaken by their descendants.

In this garden there are roses in both side borders. On the left-hand side, looking down the garden, the fence is covered with three climbers in shades of pink, 'Zephirine Drouhin', 'Bantry Bay' and the single-flowered 'Summer Wine'. In front of these climbers is a line of bush roses, beginning with white 'Iceberg', then 'Peace' (because although seen so often, it does have very lovely flowers), then a darker pink, perhaps 'Fragant Cloud', and finally, at the end of the garden, 'Madame Isaac Pereire' which is taller than the others, with abundant dark pink flowers and a strong scent.

The roses look best in blocks of one colour, rather than planted singly, so use, for example, four 'Iceberg', followed by two 'Peace' then three 'Fragrant Cloud' and a single 'Madame Isaac Pereire'. All the roses are underplanted with *Nepeta × faassenii* (catmint). This perennial has grey-green leaves with a smell that is unobtrusive to humans but seems to have a strange fascination for some cats. On the whole the plant seems to survive their attentions, and grows quite densely, providing it is cut back each spring. It makes a very good foil for roses. It is dense enough to obscure their less attractive woody stems, and is soft enough, both in colour and shape, to offset the flowers to perfection.

In the far corners of the garden, the bed is wider where the path echoes the geometric shape of the central pond. Here there is room for a cluster of larger scented shrubs, and this would be an ideal situation for one of the species of *Buddleia*. The familiar butterfly bush, *B. davidii*, has many named varieties, with flowers in all the shades of blue and purple as well as in white. 'Black Knight' has a particularly attractive rich, dark colour that would look wonderful beside the dark pink roses. *B. davidii* flowers on new growth, which is vigorous, so it should be pruned in early spring before growth begins. This shrub or small tree is easily grown against a wall by cutting it back to a low trunk (rather like pollarding) and then tying back or cutting out branches that would hang too far across the path. The direction of growth can be governed to some extent by pruning back to a bud pointing in the direction that you want a branch to grow, in the same way as a rose bush is treated.

B. davidii is very attractive to butterflies, and many people plant them both to enjoy their warm, sweet scent and in the hope of attracting these beautiful insects. In fact this really only works if there are butterflies already in the area, and the best way of covering your butterfly bush with a cloud of butterflies is to grow the food plant chosen by their caterpillars as well. This is a less popular strategy with many gardeners, because several of the most attractive butterflies depend, in their larval stage, on plant species which are less than desirable, notably stinging nettles.

Under the arching branches of the buddleia, towards the end fence of the garden, is a *Philadelphus* hybrid, 'Belle Etoile'. All the species and hybrids of *Philadelphus* are perfumed, some more strongly than others. They have creamy white flowers in early summer and a distinctive scent, not liked by all, which is strongest in the evening. 'Belle Etoile' is a good variety for a small garden because it is fairly compact in shape and, if pruned hard after flowering each year, will not get too big.

The opposite border is planted in a similar way, but with roses in shades of cream and yellow. 'Golden Showers' is a good yellow climber, and the colour of a rose, incidentally, that is believed to have been introduced from Persia. The bushes below them are 'Pascali', followed by 'St Hugh's', then a bronze colour, perhaps 'Adolph Horstmann', and finally the modern shrub 'Frühlingsgold'. This last is not repeat flowering, but the sweet fragrance and profusion of flowering in early summer is enough to justify its choice. In the corner bed at the end of the yellow roses is another species of *Buddleia*.

Buddleia globosa, which is also scented, has spherical orange flowers, like bright pom-poms, and is much loved by bees. Interestingly, the much commoner *B. davidii* is the later introduction of the two, brought to Europe from China at the very end of the last century, by which time *B. globosa*, originally from South America, had been grown in Europe for more than a hundred years. Although they are closely related, the *B. globosa* grows much less vigorously. When young, it needs pruning to establish a suitably shaped framework of branches but, after this, it requires very little attention.

Beside this buddleia, in the equivalent position to the philadelphus on the opposite side of the garden, is a rosemary bush, *Rosmarinus officinalis*. The young shoots of rosemary grow straight upright and the pale undersides of its leaves give the bush almost a look of vertical stripes. It also tends to collapse forward as it grows, however, and looks best when it is trimmed each year in the spring as the new growth begins. It can also be tied and trained as a wall shrub. The aroma of the foliage is strong and very distinctive and, as it is a vigorous shrub, there will always be plenty to cut for drying, cooking or using to scent a fire. Like parsley, it is one of those herbs that is said to grow best in female-dominated households but, in fact, it is an easy-tempered plant and will do well enough anywhere. All it asks is a soil which drains well and does not become waterlogged in winter.

At the end of the garden is a fan-trained fig tree, completely covering the wall with its thick, dark leaves and, in a good summer, bearing luscious fruit. In all except the warmest parts of the country, the fig must be regarded as half-hardy. It can only be grown on the sunniest wall, and even then it will need some protection against frost in winter. It is a lush and handsome tree, however, when circumstances allow it. Fig trees become very large and leafy, but because they do not fruit well if they are allowed to develop a wide-ranging root system they should always be restricted by a submerged container or planted, like this one, in a narrow bed between a wall and a solid, unbroken path.

Although fig trees grown in warmer climates may produce as many as three crops in a year, in cool temperate areas only one crop will ripen, and that is somewhat dependent on the vagaries of the weather. Tiny fruits are produced in late summer on the previous year's growth, and these overwinter and ripen the following summer. They are damaged by frost but can be protected by an armful of straw or bracken, held around the branch with wide-mesh plastic netting. A second crop of fruits will appear on the new growth, but this has no chance whatever of ripening and should be removed in the autumn so that all the

A very different atmosphere is created by a pool constructed at the crossing of two paths.

tree's energies can be devoted to the one crop which you hope to eat.

Growing a fig tree is rather an ambitious project, and it could be replaced by a pair of fan- or espalier-trained fruit trees, perhaps dessert cherries or plums, or by a line of cordons.

Walking away from the fruit tree you can either continue and complete the circuit of the perimeter pathway or walk back towards the house through the sunken garden, which can be entered via two steps at either end. In summer there are pots on these steps, with scented

Santolina chamaecyparissus *(cotton lavender) used as an edging for a border of plants with blue-grey foliage.*

species of *Pelargonium*, for example *P. graveolens*, *P. crispum* and *P. tomentosum*. Most pelargoniums have aromatic leaves; indeed the characteristic smell of some, including the zonal hybrids often wrongly called geraniums, is so strong as to be unpleasant. There are other species and hybrids, however, with rather smaller and less conspicuous flowers and deeply lobed aromatic and sometimes variegated leaves, giving between them an amazing range of scents, including orange, lemon, peppermint, almond, apple, pine, rose and many more. They are generally South African in origin and are grown in temperate climates as conservatory or house plants. They thrive in strong light and thoroughly welcome a few months outside in the summer sun. The extra vigour of their growth outdoors is indicated by foliage that is much darker, denser and generally healthier than that of plants indoors, but since they are not hardy, winter inside and summer out suits them very well. They grow very easily from cuttings.

Plants with scented foliage almost inevitably provide stimulation for the sense of touch as well as that of smell because their perfumes are released most strongly when they are disturbed or crushed. But there are other plants which are a pleasure to handle, particularly those with hairy or furry leaves. The best known of these is surely *Stachys lanata*, which has a host of common names referring to its texture, likening it to the

ears or tongue of several animals, notably the donkey or lamb. It is undoubtedly very hard to resist the urge to finger the silky, silvery leaves, and even harder to do so in this case because it is grown in the herbaceous bed, which is one step up from the sunken garden and so within easy reach.

On each side of the steps nearer the house there is another, very touchable plant, the weeping pussy willow (*Salix caprea*), sometimes called the Kilmarnock willow. This is a small tree with a head of weeping branches which carry grey catkins in the spring, turning to yellow as they mature. They are seen at various heights between 1m and 2.7m (4–9ft) and, as they grow, the head increases in size but the height does not greatly change. They can be very beautiful small trees. The shape is achieved by grafting, and because the head is sometimes fuller on one side than the other, it is best to see the young tree before buying it, if possible, to make sure that it has an even crown of branches. If you do have a plant which is one-sided, plant it with the fuller side facing the prevailing wind, if

Grass, stone paving and brilliant annuals alternating within a rectangular framework in the Pond Garden at Hampton Court.

any; this additional protection may encourage more branches to grow on the thin side. These willows do not, like many of their relatives, have very wide-reaching roots. They do, however, thrive best when they get plenty of water in the summer, so dig in plenty of water-retaining compost before planting and give extra water whenever the weather is dry.

In the herbaceous bed there are several plants with grey aromatic foliage, grown generally for the colouring or appearance of their leaves rather than for their flowers. *Artemisia absinthium* 'Lambrook Silver' has deeply divided leaves, very pale in colour and sharply aromatic. The herb tarragon is another species of the same genus. Rue is also grey-leaved and *Ruta graveolens* 'Jackman's Blue', which is rather more compact than the species, is the variety most often grown. *Tanacetum haradjanii* has sharply aromatic leaves which are so finely divided that they look almost like feathers. It has flowers like an over-sized groundsel, and many gar-deners, preferring the foliage alone,

The construction of a garden depicted in a sixteenth-century Mughal manuscript. Water from the canal pours into a raised tank and there are citrus fruits and pomegranates growing against the walls as well as attendant birds to delight the eye and ear.

remove these when the buds form. *Helichrysum serotinum*, the curry plant, is often given the same treatment, and this too does well in a border like this. Its name gives away the distinctive smell of its foliage.

Most of these grey-leaved plants originate from southern Europe or beyond, and although they are hardy enough they do grow best on well-drained soil. In particular they are vulnerable if their roots become waterlogged in winter, so a slightly raised bed, such as this step down into the sunken garden, would be an ideal position.

Grey-leaved plants are invaluable in a large herbaceous border as a neutral foil for more brightly coloured flowers, and in this narrow border they make a perfect background for more striking species such as lilies, iris and some of the more strongly scented annuals, including stocks, verbena and sweet peas. Lilies are generally hardy bulbs which need good drainage to prevent fungal diseases, so again this is an ideal situation. There are literally hundreds of suitable species and varieties of lilies. One very fragrant favourite is *Lilium regale* which has huge and impressive flowers towards the end of summer. *Lilium* × *maculatum* is a group of hybrids, in colours ranging from yellow to red-brown, that are reliable and among the easiest to grow, reaching no more than one metre (a little over 3ft) in height, an ideal size for this situation.

The bearded irises can also be found in almost every colour under the sun. They grow from rhizomes and do best if they are divided every few years. The flowers are large and dramatic and the hybrid 'Jane Phillips', which is a pale blue and softly scented, would look good with the yellow colours of the lilies.

Acidanthera bicolor murielae is a white-flowered corm which extends the season of the border by flowering into early autumn. The corms will not survive the winter and should be lifted after flowering except in the very mildest areas.

The four beds in the sunken garden are devoted to bulbs and annuals. In the spring there are hyacinths. The variety 'City of Haarlem' is sometimes described as yellow but is really more like a dark cream, a wonderful colour and highly scented. They are surrounded by blue and yellow winter-flowering pansies and a pale blue variety of the tiny *Iris reticulata*, called 'Cantab'. The scent of these hyacinths (which should be lifted and stored rather than left in the ground), is so pervasive that it is better not mixed with any other spring fragrance; for another year, the jonquil (*Narcissus jonquilla* 'Trevithian') is equally powerful.

For summer planting there is, in the two larger beds, a mixture of the tobacco plant, *Nicotiana alata*, and *Heliotropium peruvianum* 'Royal Marine'. There are a number of varieties of *N. alata* in single or mixed colours, although many believe the species is the most fragrant. One particularly attractive and still very fragrant variety is 'Lime Green' which has pale yellowish green flowers which fill the garden with evening perfume and contrast in colour with the dark, almost purple flowers of the heliotrope.

The smaller beds have tall wigwams of sweet peas, surrounded by basil which is both pleasantly aromatic in the summer garden and invaluable in the kitchen. Its sharp smell is the perfect foil to the sweet peas. There is something of a convention that sweet peas are grown as part of the vegetable garden because the flowers are picked with such frequency that the plants are spoiled for the flower garden. They certainly need regular picking, because once they have set seed they will stop flowering, and it is a great pleasure, in a small garden, to be able to pick freely for once, knowing that it is not spoiling the display, but is essential for its development. In fact, the next flush of flowers opens so soon that the plants are left with unadorned foliage for only a matter of hours. The blue varieties are thought to have the best scent, and 'Noel Sutton', 'Leamington' and 'Evensong' are all a good choice. If you want a mixture of colours, the scent is perhaps not quite as good but still more than adequate.

The pebble canals across the sunken garden are planted with two species of mint, *Mentha pulegium*, or pennyroyal, and *M. requienii*, or Corsican mint. Neither of these bear much obvious resemblance to the culinary spearmint. Both are creeping plants which will reach only a few centimetres in height and both are mildly peppermint in fragrance when trodden on. Their tiny leaves make pools of green amongst the cobbles.

THE GARDEN OF OPPOSITES

This garden combines two different styles in a long, narrow plot. The part nearest the house is formal, with a paved terrace and path enclosing a semi-circular, closely clipped lawn. Placed round the lawn are six pots, each holding a conical silver privet, and round the whole D-shape is a smooth, dark green hedge, broken at the centre by a trellis archway giving a view to the bottom of the garden. Through the arch the garden is much softer and wilder, with slightly longer grass, naturally shaped shrubs and colourful flowers. On the right-hand side is a small stream trickling past a line of shrubs and trees and into a small pond. Behind the pond, and forming the focus of the garden, is a piece of sculpture or a sundial against a background of dark green holly trees and a small mixed coppice. There are informally arranged water-loving plants round the pond, and a bark-chip path winds through the trees, with a shady seat beside it, emerging on the other side of the pond. On this side of the garden there is a mixed border of pink and white flowering shrubs and plants, ending back at the clipped hedge near the house in a small rose garden. This continues the colour scheme, with several varieties at different heights to use the vertical space to full advantage.

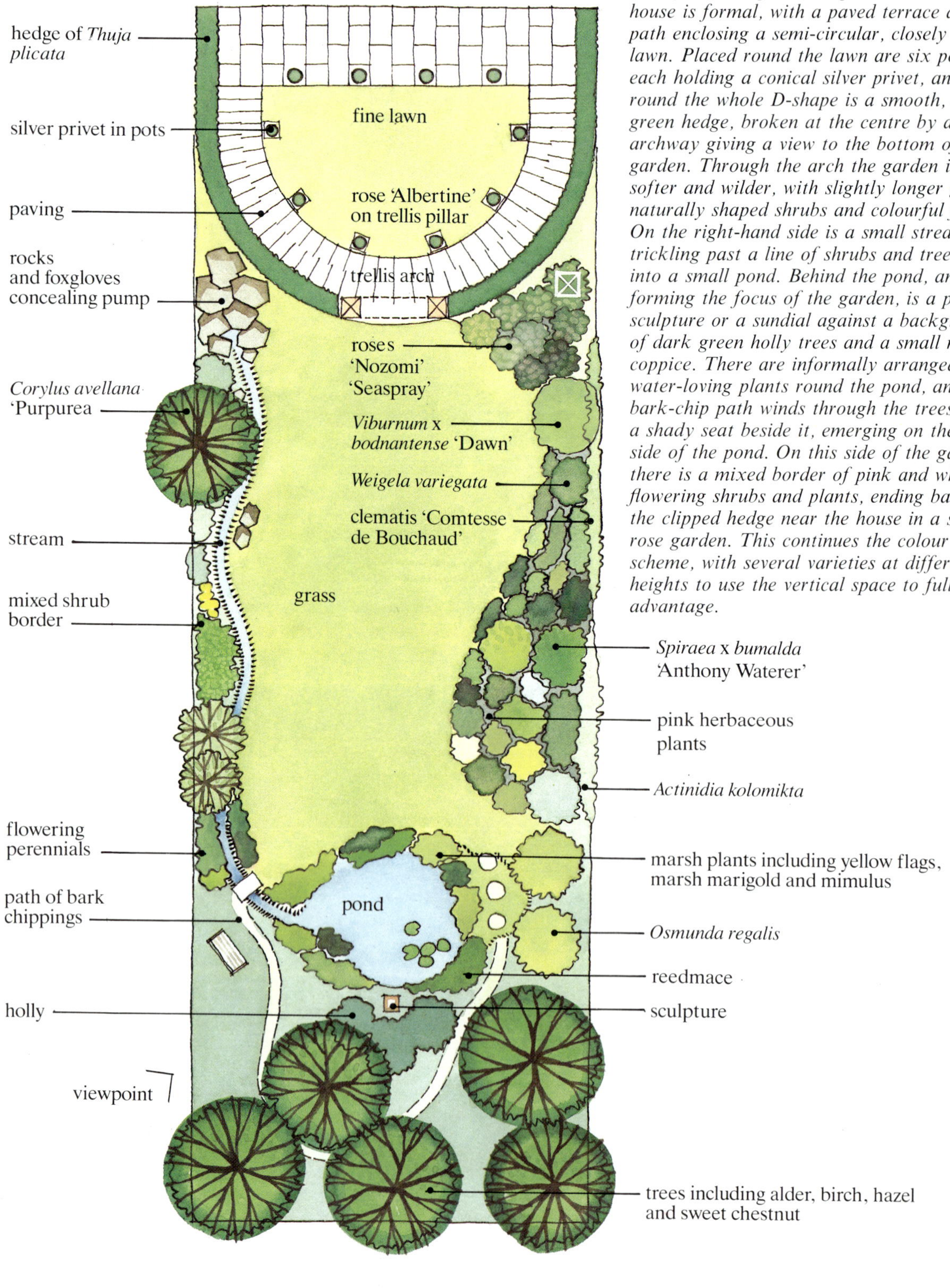

This garden uses two quite different historic styles to solve a problem that faces very many gardeners living in or around towns, namely a garden that is very long in proportion to its width. It is not just modern estates that suffer from this kind of garden; for at least the last hundred years builders and land speculators have crammed houses as closely together as they could manage. The house in this case is a modern one; mock Georgian, built in the 1960s, with a symmetrical façade and a rectangular garden about 27m (90ft) long and 9m (30ft) wide.

The first part of the garden is very formal, which matches the mood of the surrounding architecture. There is a straight paved terrace right along the back of the house, and beyond this a semicircular lawn which was sown with what is usually called a 'high-quality lawn mixture'. This means it can be closely mown to a surface approaching a bowling green but will not survive the onslaught of children and dogs, who need a grass mixture which will take more wear.

At regular intervals round the lawn there are six stone-finish pots, simple in their design, and each holding a silver privet trimmed to a neat cone shape. There is then a paved path all the way round. The whole D-shape is enclosed by a smooth, dark green hedge, about 1.4m (4ft 6in) high, which is broken at the centre by a fairly wide trellis archway giving a view to the bottom of the garden.

The hedge is *Thuja plicata*, which is a fairly fast-growing conifer although nothing like as vigorous as the ubiquitous × *Cupressocyparis leylandii*. It is hardy, however, and has an extremely good, dark colour which makes it ideal for this particular garden where the contrasts between the different shades in the hedge, the grass, and the privets are important. When planting the hedge, the ground should be prepared thoroughly (see page 173). Use a curving hosepipe to mark the

The view through a formal trellis arch leads the eye down the garden. The anticipation of something new to look at, somewhere waiting to be explored, is perhaps increased by the circuitous journey of the path round the lawn before it goes under the arch.

Converging avenues in the gardens of Chiswick House in west London.

exact line the hedge must follow and set the young plants about 60cm (2ft) apart. When the hedge has reached the right height, about 1.4m (4ft 6in), cut the leader shoot. From then on just trim the sides of the hedge so that it holds a proper shape. When a conifer hedge is well established it is generally possible to get away with cutting it once only each year, but in this garden the close, neat appearance of the hedge is important and it may need a second trim towards the end of the summer. As always, the hedge needs to be cut so that it is slightly wider at the base than it is at the top to prevent the upper part of the hedge from overshadowing the branches beneath. Without enough light, the lower part of the hedge will put on less new growth and end up looking rather uneven or, in the worst cases, bald.

It is particularly important in a formal garden like this that the hedge is kept exactly level and regular, and it is not possible to do this consistently by eye alone. Whenever the hedge is cut, use a hosepipe to mark the curved line of the base and a horizontal string stretched over the hedge as a guide for the top. (Screw small hooks into the fence and the arch and tie the string to these whenever you cut the hedge.) Finally, trim up the hedge, sloping it slightly inward.

In a way, this first part of the garden is a modern echo of a feature from the very grand style of gardening that developed in seventeenth-century France. A number of long avenues were constructed, often lined with trees, and these converged on to a semicircular hedged arena to form a pattern called a *patte d'oie* or 'goose-foot'. This modern garden is clearly quite different in very many ways – it has no

Formal hedging used to divide a garden into a series of 'rooms' each with an individual style and character.

canals, no fountains, no classical statues and only one humble archway instead of half a dozen avenues each with its own immaculate vista. But in the same way as its larger and grander ancestor, it does mirror the architecture of the house with a formal shape, and so serves to focus the first part of the garden upon the house, leaving a feeling that somewhere still to be explored lies beyond.

Standing on the terrace or at a window in the house and looking through the arch, there is a glimpse of a much wilder garden – a piece of the countryside captured for the town. At the bottom of this garden, as far away as the eye can see, there is even woodland, with glossy dark holly trees forming the backdrop for a small sculpture.

As one walks through the arch there is a complete change of mood and atmosphere. This second garden is much softer, much wilder; the grass in the lawn is left a little longer and there are naturalized spring bulbs, such as winter aconites and daffodils. It is full of plants and colour and interesting features to look at and enjoy.

On the right-hand side there is a small stream which trickles down the garden and into a pond. The pump that drives it is concealed by rocks and by clusters of white and purple foxgloves. Small-scale circulating systems of this kind are fortunately not as complex to install as they are rewarding to look at. The side of the garden here needs to be banked up

slightly, so that the stream flows down into the pond and the water can then be pumped back up through a buried pipe.

Alongside the stream as it flows down the garden, and concealing the fence, is a line of shrubs and trees. There is a philadelphus, a variety such as 'Belle Etoile', which has lovely arching sprays of creamy-white scented flowers and grows to about 1.5m (5ft) in height. Then a tree, *Acer palmatum* 'Atropurpureum', which has purple foliage. Other purple-leaved shrubs are *Berberis thunbergii atropurpurea*, *Cotinus coggygria* 'Royal Purple' and *Corylus maxima* 'Purpurea' which has dense foliage with large leaves and will grow almost as tall as the acer. Because the purple colour is most striking in new growth it should be pruned hard after flowering every couple of years. In contrast, there is the grey foliage of *Senecio laxifolius*, also pruned hard to encourage new growth, and *Eucalyptus gunnii*. The eucalyptus is really a fast-growing tree, but if it is cut back each March, in a pruning process that is rather like a form of annual coppicing, all its new growth comes from ground level which will give it the shape of a shrub. It can grow as much as 1.2–1.8m (4–6ft) in a season and any particularly vigorous upright shoots should be cut back at the tips to maintain the shrubby shape.

Farther down the garden there is a

An informal garden stream with a fringe of Osmunda regalis *and other farms.*

Wood chips edged with logs make a good pathway into the marshy corner of the garden.

snowberry (*Symphoricarpos rivularis*) and a couple of small, shrubby willows (*Salix lanata*) with their grey leaves and lovely 'pussy willow' flowers in spring. Then, a dramatic clump of *Acanthus mollis latifolius* against the fence and clusters of astilbe (such as 'Rheinland' or 'Peach Blossom') in the damp soil round the stream as it turns left under a simple stone slab bridge into the pond.

This pond, with the sculpture and hollies behind it, is the focus of the garden when it is seen through the arch from the house. It is more or less round in shape, with soft, boggy edges. The effect round the pond is very natural and uses mostly wild plants such as yellow 'flags' (*Iris pseudocorus*), water forget-me-not (*Myosotis palustris*), kingcups (*Caltha palustris*) and water mint (*Mentha aquatica*) beside bog-loving plants such as meadowsweet (*Filipendula ulmaria*), lady's smock or cuckoo flower (*Cardamine pratensis*) and creeping Jenny (*Lysimachia nummularia*). Nevertheless this borrowing and improving of nature for the sake of the garden inevitably involves a certain amount of very subtle management. For example, the water level in the bog needs watching, so that it neither dries out in the summer nor becomes waterlogged in the winter; the plants themselves are here arranged and clustered to give the best effect.

Potentially the sculpture behind the pond poses a problem. Statuary generally is associated with large and rather grand gardens and in small gardens there are too many gnomes and nymphs already to wish to add to their number. However, its position in this garden is an ideal place to display a statue or, perhaps better still, a small piece of modern sculpture, for a gardener who has such a thing and wishes to look at it. The statues offered in many garden centres are often poor copies of figures that looked much better in their original setting. So proceed with care, or settle for something simpler like a sundial or an urn, or even let the hollies stand alone.

The woodland at the end of the garden is planted with birch, alder, hazel and sweet chestnut. These should be put in fairly close together (say about 1.2m/4ft apart) because it is always likely that some trees will fail, and if they do all thrive they can be thinned later. A dense thicket of trees also looks better when the trees are young, before the woodland is properly established. Beneath the trees plant bluebells and wood anemones with primroses and lesser celandines at the fringes, but bear in mind that, although tempting, it is illegal to stock your own woodland by digging up plants from the countryside. There are nurserymen who specialize in native plants and sell all these.

On the right-hand side of the wood there is a seat which makes a shady place to sit in summer and enjoy the rest of the garden. A narrow path, surfaced with bark chippings and lined with small logs, winds past it and on between the trees. On the other side of the garden the path emerges from the wood between huge clumps of reedmace and *Osmunda regalis*, the royal or king fern. Both these are large

Low box hedging and square pots used to divide a narrow lawn into two parts.

and rather dramatic waterside plants, with the reedmace and its familiar bulrushes reaching about 1.2m (4ft) in height, and the king fern a little taller. In the wild the king fern can grow as tall as 3m (10ft), but when cultivated it is generally smaller. In either case it is a handsome plant with its striking rust-brown spore capsules, and deserves greater popularity. When these two plants establish themselves and the clumps expand, they will closely surround the winding path as it emerges from the wood and over a couple of stepping stones in the bog, back into the garden. The need almost to push your way through this foliage creates a feeling of stepping from one place into another, and so makes the garden feel more spacious, more adventurous, more a place to walk round and to explore.

Throughout the summer, one of the best reasons for sitting on the woodland seat and looking back towards the house is the view of the small rose garden. Rose beds in small gardens can be a problem to arrange; the flowers undoubtedly look their best in fairly large swathes of one colour or even of a single variety. Because mixed beds do not have nearly such a strong impact the gardener with a small garden has to face a difficult decision: one variety or a less dramatic mixture. Even then a small rose bed may lack effect, just because it is not big enough for the flowers to show their best. In this garden there is a tiny rose bed, planted with three varieties – all pale pink – but the bed is a mass of colour because the plants are of different heights, and so use the vertical space to full advantage. The flowers cascade like a fountain from a towering pillar at the back of the bed, right down to the ground.

Roses come in all shapes and sizes (see page 136), and using the full range makes the best of a small space. In this bed there is an 'Albertine' climbing up a pillar which is built in the same form as the trellis arch. 'Albertine' is not repeat flowering but keeps its popularity with the astonishing mass of flowers in its one flush of bloom. Below this there are several weeping standards of a variety called 'Nozomi'. The arching and trailing branches of these weeping standards are ideal for a three-dimensional arrangement of this sort, and a number of varieties can be bought budded on to standard stems of different heights. Below that there is a floribunda, 'Seaspray', and close to the soil a prostrate or ground-cover rose, again 'Nozomi'.

Walking on down the garden, between the rose bed and the great clumps of osmunda, there is a mixed bed with climbers on the fence behind it and shrubs with herbaceous perennials in the foreground. This border has a theme colour – pink. White is, perhaps, the most popular choice for a single-colour bed or border, but other colours are equally effective. In this case the pink flowers in the mixed border echo the colour of the rose bed.

The first shrub is *Viburnum* × *bodnantense* 'Dawn', which has amazingly scented pink flowers on its bare branches in winter, before the leaves emerge in the spring. The smell of it on a depressing winter's day seems like a minor miracle and makes a trip down the garden worthwhile. After a few years, when the viburnum is well established, plant a pink clematis (such as 'Comtesse de Bouchaud') behind and to one side of it, so that the clematis grows up and over the summer foliage of the viburnum, transforming the rather dull leaves and looking as though the shrub has burst into flower again. It is quite easy to get this effect of second flowering using a hybrid clematis, because it will flower on new growth. This

Opposite: *A herbaceous border in summer. Different varieties of delphinium in white and shades of blue against a background of climbing roses.*

Below: *Banked roses in shades of pink: 'Nozomi', 'The Fairy', 'Angelina' and 'Silver Jubilee'.*

Mixed planting, including species of Geranium *and* Primula *and ferns, gives this pond a natural look and a rural atmosphere.*

means that they are pruned back almost to ground level in early spring and will make all their growth for late summer blossoms after the viburnum has finished flowering. An established shrub will not be smothered by a single year's growth of the clematis in the way that it might by a rampant species type, such as *C. montana*, which flowers on short shoots from earlier growth and will not flower at all if it is cut back annually.

In the rest of the border there are flowering shrubs, such as *Spiraea* × *bumalda* 'Anthony Waterer', one of the many varieties of shrubby *Potentilla*, *Weigela florida* 'Variegata' and, in warmer areas, varieties of *Cistus* or rock rose. In front of the shrubs there is a range of herbaceous perennials chosen for their colour and height, but also so that there is something to look good in the border from spring until autumn. (See page 140 for a plant grid that makes this planning easier.) Not all the plants need be herbaceous perennials; the half-hardy spider flower (*Cleome spinosa*) is a striking, tall plant that can be grown each year from seed. There is also room to put clumps of spring bulbs between the perennials so that the fading growth of the bulbs is camouflaged by the new growth of the perennials.

Some plants are chosen for their leaves as well as for their flowers – the pink 'Chinese' peonies (varieties and hybrids of *Paeonia lactiflora*) for example – have beautiful flowers in early summer and leave behind straight stems that do not need tying, with attractive leaves that last into the autumn. The same is true of the *Bergenia cordifolia* that is planted in several places at the front of the border, especially when the leaves are offset by the delicate white mass of one of the species of *Gypsophila*. This was one of the many plant combinations suggested or recommended by Gertrude Jekyll.

One of the great faults of herbaceous borders in many small gardens is that they have a ring of brown earth around each plant. Borders should look full. In the early years of their life there will undoubtedly be gaps as shrubs and perennials begin to grow, but these should be filled with annuals and bedding plants until the real residents of the bed mature enough to do the job themselves.

Borders like this also need to look fairly bulky. Although the plants at the front are shorter than the ones at the back, none of them are the ground creepers that are sometimes seen, and further back in the bed there are some big, tall plants. These blend into the climbers on the fence to give a border full of life and colour.

Beds like this require regular attention if they are to be successful and, indeed, this whole garden contains many of the elements that every gardener knows mean work – lawns, hedges, pond and borders.

A very formal pond, offset by a lushly planted herbaceous border.

THE ITALIAN WATER GARDEN

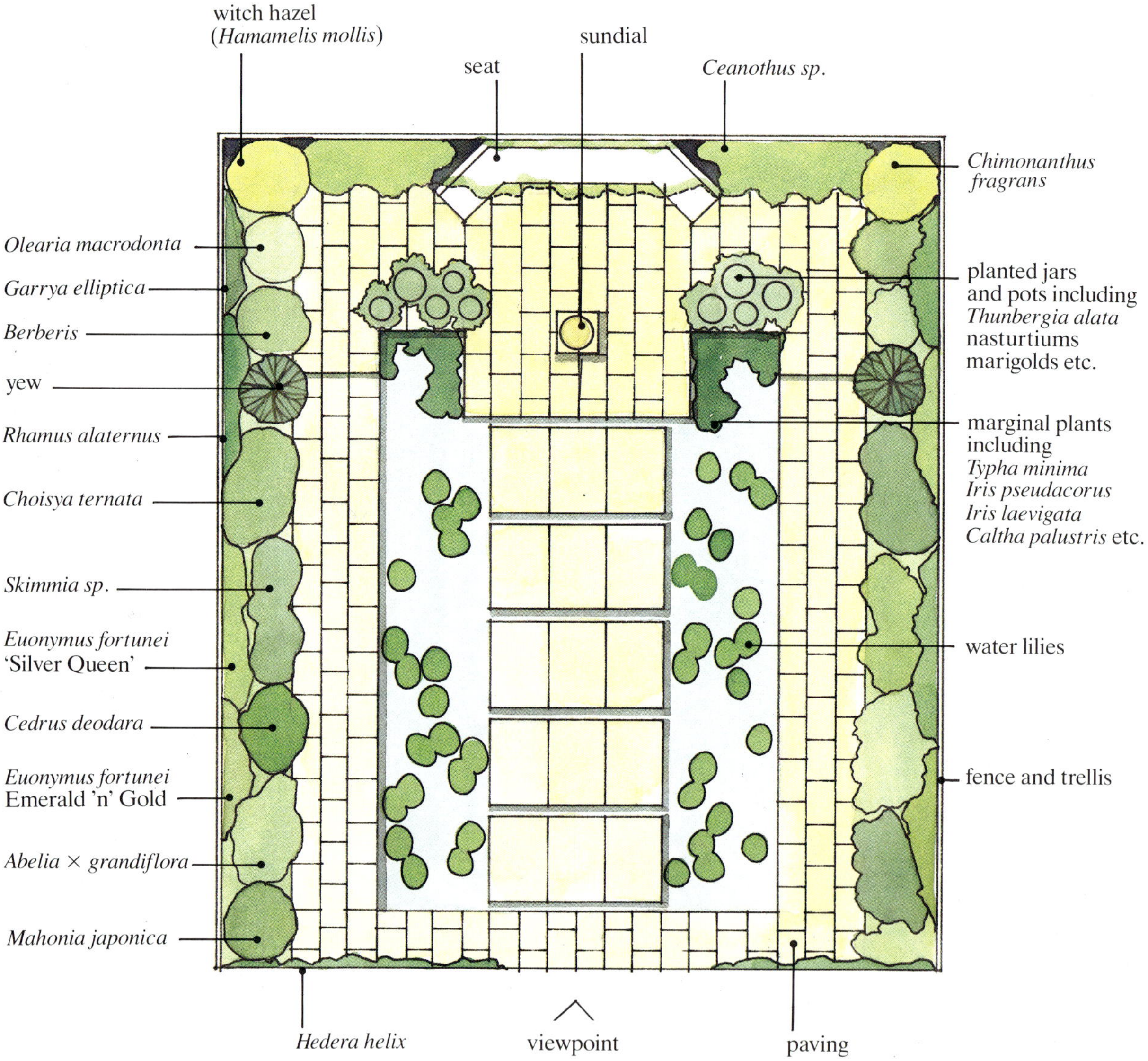

This very symmetrical garden is reminiscent of the formal waterways built on a much grander scale in European gardens of the seventeenth century. Its major feature is the large area of open water, with ornamental fish occasionally visible, but much of its character also comes from the detailed construction of the wooden seat, trellis and tubs in which a simple repeated design is used throughout. Looking down the garden, a bridge of giant stones leads across the pool to a sundial and the seat against the end wall. All the paving is of honey-coloured slabs, made from concrete but in different sizes and textures. On the surface of the water there are water lilies and on an underwater shelf on both sides of the end of the pool there are closely grown marginal plants including rushes and iris. Behind these are pots of brightly coloured flowers in shades of orange and yellow to echo the variegated foliage of the shrubs in the border along each side. Above and around the seat, linking the two sides of the garden, there is an evergreen ceanothus.

RI

This is a very symmetrical garden, with long, straight rectangles of water reminiscent in some ways of the formal waterways that were built on a much grander scale in the European gardens of the seventeenth century. It has in it, in fact, rather more water than soil, which makes it an unusual garden with a great deal of character and atmosphere. Although the inspiration behind it is from the past, it is built using undisguisedly modern materials and would be a suitable garden for a contemporary house, a town house perhaps, which has similarly strong architectural lines and, generally speaking, only a narrow rectangular plot on which to make a garden. It is also a garden which depends in part on the careful construction of the wooden seat, trellis and tubs, in which a simple repeated design is used throughout, giving some unity to the whole effect.

Looking down the garden, a bridge of giant stones leads across the pool to a

A water garden in Ireland inspired by the classic Italian style.

sundial and a large, elegant seat, which stands against the end wall and is framed by wall shrubs. Structurally, the pool is built in two separate units, so that the 'stepping stones' are actually set on to solid ground. The bridge effect is created by setting the stones 10cm (4in) or so apart and cutting down between them to make a channel, into which the water on each side can overflow. The slabs are set to overhang the water so that the path appears almost to float. It is, however,

extremely stable, making a wide, safe walkway down the garden.

All the paving is concrete, using square slabs of a single pale colour which tones with the house, in this case a light yellow honey colour; and to reinforce the clear, long, rectangular shape of the design, the paving is laid with the joints in line. The distinction between the paving round the pool and the bridge across the water is emphasized by using slabs of different textures on each. Around the sides the paving is in riven slabs, which are made to resemble the partially eroded surface of certain sedimentary rocks, and across the pool it is in textured slabs which are made so that the stony aggregate they contain is exposed on the upper surface. Both these slabs have a rough finish and are much less slippery than those with a smooth surface, which is no bad thing in a garden with so much water. When choosing concrete slabs, or for that matter any paving, it is wise to see it both wet and dry because the colour variation is sometimes surprisingly great. A subtle shade of terracotta can be transformed by a shower of rain into a livid shade of red.

At the far end of the pool, on both sides, there is an underwater shelf to hold marginal plants. These are grown in plastic baskets, clustered closely together to make a dense fringe of foliage around the step and including *Typha minima* which is a kind of dwarf bulrush with short, fat seed heads, unlike the typical reedmace. There is also a variegated form of the common yellow flag, *Iris pseudocorus* 'Variegata', with brightly striped yellow leaves, as straight and sharp as a sword, and large yellow flowers in early summer. The straight leaves of these plants contrast with the lusher foliage of *Sagittaria sagittifolia*, which has white flowers (double in the variety 'Flore Pleno'), and a couple of types of kingcup, *Caltha palustris*. 'Alba' has single white flowers with a yellow centre and 'Plena' is the familiar brilliant yellow of the species but with double flowers.

The pool itself is large enough to hold a couple of water lilies, species and hybrids of *Nymphaea*, perhaps × *Marliacea* 'Albida' or × 'Sunrise'. It is also a good situation for some fish which, in this large volume of water, should reach a good size. The fish kept in ponds are generally goldfish and their close relations, but whereas a goldfish the size of your little finger remains a matter for children and fairgrounds, there is a definite excitement in catching a glimpse of a larger fish as it flicks silently from beneath the lily pads. Once settled they are fairly hardy and will breed when they are 12–13cm (about 5in) long. They are unheeding parents who will cheerfully consume their own offspring, so the survival rate of the fry depends largely on there being enough vegetation in the pond to provide hiding places for the baby fish until they are too large to make a mouthful.

The amount of clear water surface that is visible in a pool has a very considerable effect on the character and atmosphere of any garden in which water plays a part. In this pool it is very important not to let the foliage of the lilies take over and smother the surface with leaves. The calm reflecting surface of still water is part of the beauty and charm in any garden and an important part of the character of this one, so there must always be enough clear water to reflect the shrubs and trellis that enclose the garden.

For an entirely different effect, install a line of angled fountains down each outside edge of the pool, set to play towards the central bridge, so that they make an enclosing archway of spray. The fountain nozzles should be set just below the overhanging rim of the paving and the force of the water should be calculated with some care, because the object is to walk over the bridge between symmetrical arching fountains, not to have a shower. In addition, high fountains catch the wind and the water can be blown right out of the pool, which must eventually mean topping it up because the fountain adds nothing to the volume but only circulates the water that is there. Water lilies do much better in still water, although the fish will welcome the oxygen introduced by the splashing. The atmosphere of the garden with fountains would be quite different, much livelier and more dramatic, but without the tranquillity created by still reflecting water.

Walking down the garden, you step from the bridge on to a tongue of paving that cuts into the pool. On this there is a sundial and a number of pots, made in the same colour as the paving, and planted according to the season. These planted containers are the brightest splash of

Right: *Terracotta pots match the brickwork and contrast with the paving round this rectangular pond. Mixed shrubby planting around the garden and marginals at the edge of the pond soften the lines and lessen the formality of the atmosphere.*

Opposite: *Arched fountains enliven the water in a Moorish garden.*

colour in the summer garden, containing a variety of species, all with flowers of one colour range. In this case, the predominant colour is yellow-orange, with daffodils and wallflowers in the spring, followed by *Thunbergia alata* (sometimes called 'black-eyed Susan'), growing up a narrow cane wigwam, and nasturtiums tumbling down the sides. The smaller jars have English or pot marigolds (*Calendula officinalis*, also called Scotch or common marigolds), yellow antirrhinums, *Limnanthes douglasii*, *Alyssum saxatile* and the yellow-leaved and -flowered creeping Jenny (*Lysimachia nummularia* 'Aurea'). These last two are perennials and can be left round the edge of the pots from one year to the next. It is important to feed them well if you do this, however, and also to scrape out some of the compost from the centre of the pot and replace it when changing the bulbs and annuals.

One of the great advantages of container planting is that you can completely change the colour scheme from one year to the next. An alternative scheme could be pink, including tulips and primulas followed by species of *Impatiens*, *Pelargonium*, *Petunia* and *Verbena*. Verbena is a lovely half-hardy annual for containers and hanging baskets, with bright, and fairly long-lasting flowers. The stems do not quite trail, but neither do they grow upright, so it forms a wild, spiky coronet of colour round the pot.

Annual climbers, such as *Thunbergia alata*, add a much-needed variety of height to container planting. This can also be achieved by raising some of the pots on suitable blocks, and in this garden the height is varied in this way, using an extra paving stone. Another useful climber in this context is morning glory (*Ipomoea rubro-caerulea*), which has stunningly beautiful flowers, most usually blue, that open each morning and have faded by the evening. The young plants are prone to fungal disease and succumb very easily if they are watered either too much or too little, but they are well worth this extra attention, and will continue to produce new flowers each day for several weeks. The ideal position for them is somewhere fairly warm and sheltered, with morning sun, rather than strong noonday heat which will wither the flowers by lunchtime.

Containers and tubs are sometimes most striking if they are planted with a single species or variety, rather than with a more conventional mixture. It makes for a hard decision, because the choice is so large, but the final effect is better, particularly in a more formal garden, where a container planted with mixed colours may introduce an incongruous cottagey look. But mixing species is often

Benches set at an angle provide a more companionable space than a straight seat. Round the bed on the left, young box plants are beginning to join into a low hedge.

A simple bench built into the design of a trellis arch.

the way to get a range of heights and a good shape to the planting; using one type alone gives a flat look that does not show the flowers at their best. Some plants can be trained or pruned into various forms to achieve this variation. For example, zonal pelargoniums can be grown as standards or half-standards by pinching out all the lateral shoots until the stem is the required height, and only then pinching out the tip to encourage it to bush out. With less flexible annuals, such as antirrhinums or schizanthus, another approach is to use an additional, second pot, smaller than the main container. When the plants are ready for bedding out, plant this pot first, half bury it in the middle of the container and then continue planting round it. For a while, when the plants are small, the second pot is visible and looks rather odd, but it is soon hidden by the growing vegetation, and the effect when the plants bloom is one of a smooth dome of flowers.

In the winter the pots can be planted with small ivies and dwarf conifers. There are many of these and the small size of modern gardens has increased their popularity. Some of them are not truly dwarf and will eventually make quite large trees, but their growth is so slow that they can safely be regarded as dwarf for many years. *Chamaecyparis lawsoniana* 'Silver Thread' is a good one for this garden. It has lovely foliage, with a touch of creamy colour in the 'thread' on the

The use of water in the classic Italian manner adds to the tranquillity of a formal design.

leaves, and a narrow conical shape, eventually reaching 1.2m (4ft). In the summer they can be moved into a shady corner or stand in the shrub border, but they must be kept well watered. This is the penalty of keeping plants in containers; because they dry out completely in weather which is quite wet enough for the same plants in open soil, they must have regular watering. An alternative to conifers, except in the coldest part of the country, is the smaller species of *Hebe*. Several of these plants are fairly hardy and very attractive, with tiny, densely packed leaves.

On each side of the garden there is a border of shrubs and, behind this, a close-boarded wooden fence, about 1.2m (4ft) high, topped by a custom-made, white-painted open trellis, taking the whole barrier to a height of 1.8m (6ft). The fence posts, topped with simple finials, stand a little higher. The trellis is not one that is made to be covered with plants, but is a decorative feature with a design which is repeated in the structure of the seat at the end of the garden. The wooden fence below it is largely obscured by shrubs.

The shrub border is mixed, but with an emphasis on evergreens, and there are a number of plants with golden or variegated leaves. There are variegated varieties of many garden species, and some are extremely bright, rather harsh even, in colour. The choice here is from softer colours, largely from plants which have streaks of cream or a touch of gold in their leaves rather than bright yellow foliage. Some variegated forms are slightly more tender than the species from which they derive, but in this garden they are planted within the shelter of the fence, so the choice remains fairly wide.

The largest species in this border are *Prunus lusitanica* and *Garrya elliptica*. Both are evergreen and, left untouched, will eventually grow to trees, but both can be kept dense and to a suitable size by pruning after flowering. The prunus has fairly large, dark green, glossy leaves and a red tinge to the bark, whereas the garrya is a paler colour, nearer sage green.

Amongst the rather smaller shrubs, the sage green is continued by another evergreen, *Olearia macrodonta*, the New Zealand holly, which has prickly holly-shaped leaves and white flowers. *Berberis darwinii* has leaves of the same shape but

A similar ground plan, with brick paving and a pond that is crowded with marginal plants, creates an entirely different atmosphere from the formal classic styles.

only a fraction the size, and accompanied by tiny yellow or orange flowers which are then followed by dark blue-black berries. There are other species of *Berberis* too. The low-growing evergreen *B. candidula* fills the front of the border, growing slowly until it reaches 80cm or so (just less than 3ft) and there is also a yellow-leaved deciduous variety, *B. thunbergii* 'Aurea', which has striking orange foliage in the autumn.

Leaves of glossy green are provided by *Choisya ternata*, sometimes called the Mexican orange blossom, by *Abelia × grandiflora*, various camellias, *Skimmia* spp., *Mahonia japonica* and *Viburnum tinus*. Choisya also has scented clusters of white flowers in early summer, but is most valuable for its solid, domed shape and clear colour. Abelia has smaller leaves, which are pleasantly pale and glossy, and carries pink-white flowers very late into autumn. It is truly only a semi-evergreen, but keeps most of its leaves through the whole winter. There are a couple of species of *Skimmia*, a shrub with a very trim, tidy shape and neat, glossy green leaves. Although there are some varieties said to be self-fertile, generally the male and female flowers are carried on separate plants and both must be planted fairly close together to get the striking red berries on the female plants in winter. One male plant will fertilize several females.

The species of *Mahonia* chosen for this border is *M. japonica*. This has beautifully scented flowers, creamy yellow in colour, which come out in late winter and sprawl over the whorls of leaves. As it matures it sometimes gets rather woody at the base, so it is a good choice for the back of a low shrub border. Another excellent winter-flowering evergreen is *Viburnum tinus*. The variegated variety has leaves with creamy yellow margins, perfect for a situation like this where they make a bright show of colour but are not too strongly gold.

Other yellow or variegated shrubs include *Rhamnus alaternus* 'Argenteo-variegata', which has similarly soft colouring but is more vigorous in growth and can be trimmed to make a taller pillar of leaves close to one of the fence posts. *Euonymus fortunei* is an ideal wall shrub, evergreen, with dense leaves, and is easily trimmed to shape. There are a number of variegated forms: 'Variegata' and 'Silver Queen' have cream or white colouring whereas 'Emerald 'n' Gold' is a much brighter yellow. The different varieties look good planted together.

The varieties of *Elaeagnus pungens* have similarly shaped leaves, but a little larger and altogether tougher and coarser-looking. But it is a dramatic shrub, particularly 'Maculata'. 'Dicksonii' and 'Variegata' are less vigorous in growth and have slightly more subdued leaves. *E. ebbingei* 'Gilt Edge' is probably the most striking.

There are many yellow and variegated conifers available, and there are two in this border. One is a particularly attractive type of yew, with a name that is something of a mouthful: *Taxus baccata* 'Fastigiata Aurea', really no more than the golden-leaved upright growing yew. There are varieties of *T. baccata* which have a brighter colour, such as 'Standishii' but these are harsh by comparison. The other conifer here is low and weeping in growth, a dwarf variety of *Cedrus deodara*, called 'Golden Horizon', which has yellow foliage which will spill over on to the path.

In the end corners of the garden there are two deciduous, winter-flowering shrubs, witch hazel (*Hamamelis mollis*) on one side and, opposite it, wintersweet, *Chimonanthus fragrans*. Both have scented yellow flowers carried on bare branches, but because witch hazel is the hardier of the two, the wintersweet should go on the sunnier side of the garden. The fragrance of wintersweet is stunning.

These two larger, rather open shrubs enclose the end fence. In the middle of them, looking back over the sundial and the pools towards the house, stands a seat. This has a decorated back in the same design as the trellis and is three-sided so that two or three people can sit comfortably in a triangle to converse, rather than being committed to a much less sociable straight line. Another way of dealing with this would be to use one bench plus two individual seats which could stand together when not in use, but be pulled out when necessary. The seats are painted white. This particular seat is not a commercial design, but although a modern teak seat from the local garden centre would create nothing like the same effect, there are a number of companies which make reproduction period garden furniture with products that would do as well. There were some wonderfully elegant garden seats made in the eighteenth century, by designers who included Thomas Chippendale, and some of these designs are still repeated, as are the simpler but equally beautiful nineteenth-century designs of Lutyens. A fairly simple modern design, painted white, would be less effective but very much cheaper and easier to find.

Against the end fence around the seat, is an evergreen ceanothus, tied and trimmed so that it grows densely, clinging to its support. There are a number of suitable varieties and hybrids, including × 'Gloire de Versailles', 'Delight', 'Autumnal Blue' and 'A. T. Stanson'. Against a fence or wall, all these can be regularly pruned to encourage dense growth, and are fairly hardy. Any damage done to the longer shoots by frost can be cut away before growth begins in spring. They do not grow well when cut into hard wood so it is important not to let a ceanothus in a position like this get too large and straggly before pruning it, but to keep it well trimmed and dense. Most varieties flower in the spring on the previous year's growth, so should have their major cut after flowering has finished, but tying in and pruning outward growing shoots or breastwood can continue as necessary right through the growing season.

Looking back at the house, there is an ivy growing up the wall, a variety of *Hedera helix* called 'Goldheart', which draws the house and garden together. It has small, pointed leaves with dark green margins and a brilliant yellow centre. Because it clings very tightly to the wall it has a generally neat appearance compared with many other varieties, and so it will not spoil the formal effect of the garden as a whole.

THE WILDERNESS GARDEN

This small L-shaped plot gives a feeling of sheltering greenery and seclusion by using trees, shrubs and plants with lush foliage and large, interesting leaf shapes planted in a raised bed to make them higher and more dramatic. From the house the view into the garden is framed by a pair of neatly clipped standard box or bay trees, their smooth formality contrasting with and emphasizing the shrubby 'wilderness' beyond. The central bed is thickly planted with trees and shrubs, including eucalyptus and sumach, with birch and corkscrew hazel round the perimeter, against the ivy-covered fence. The paving uses small, rectangular slabs which give a fairly dense texture. On the wall beyond the central bed, and hidden from the house by trees, is a small basin fed by a mask or lion water spout. The dramatic foliage, some of which is evergreen, gives the wilderness character to this town garden which also has contrasts and an element of surprise.

Since the sixteenth century, the makers of gardens have sought from time to time to explore their relationship with nature and aimed for a garden which uses and exploits its wilder side, rather than taming, restricting and enclosing it, which is what most gardening is all about. At first sight this seems a contradiction, but over the centuries there have been several ways in which the problem has been tackled. One is by using native plants to create a natural environment which will support a community of plants, insects and birds that will be a pleasure to observe. In the second half of this century this kind of gardening has been given a boost by an increasing concern for the wildlife and environments that are being destroyed by ever faster urban expansion.

Another theme that has recurred several times in garden fashion is the idea of a garden kept not naturally wild but as a 'wilderness'. In the formal gardens of the seventeenth century the wilderness was a bosquet or copse of trees interlaced with straight paths, but in the course of the next century the paths began to wind, sometimes with labyrinthine complexity. A need was felt to create, in the manicured, tidy and open landscapes of the eighteenth century, somewhere enclosed, somewhere which promised adventure and surprise. The concept was taken to its most bizarre extremes, and gardens were filled with grottoes and caves, underground passages and streams.

On the infinitely smaller scale of a twentieth-century garden there is no need to look for a wilderness as a contrast to wide vistas and open ground, but there is still the same need to feel enclosed by the garden; more so in some ways because of the threatening urban surroundings that the garden excludes. So this is a plan for a small, shady plot which uses shrubs and small trees with evergreen climbers to create just that feeling of secluded mystery.

The garden is made L-shaped by the layout of the adjacent house. A brick wall, 1.8m (6ft) high, continues the line of this house down one side of the garden, and at one point also acts as a retaining wall for the central raised bed. The other two boundaries are enclosed by a fence of the same height, made from vertical struts of wood mounted about one centimetre apart. This maintains privacy just as well as a close-boarded fence, but looks less overpoweringly solid and in a small garden feels much less claustrophobic.

Walking from the house into the garden, the view is framed by a pair of swagged pots, each holding a closely clipped, ball-shaped standard box or bay. This trimmed formality contrasts dramatically with the shrubs beyond, so emphasizing the 'wilderness'; on the return journey towards the house it also makes a frame for the doorway. The garden is paved with small, rectangular concrete slabs (about 40 × 20cm/16 × 8in). The slabs have a riven surface – that is, they are moulded on a natural stone bed – but although they are cast on stone, they are not an accurate imitation, and nor are they meant to be. They have a rough finish, which is safer than smooth-cast concrete (because it is less slippery), and a fairly pleasant appearance. Real stone would always look better, but it is much more expensive. This kind of

concrete paving is generally sold in a range of colours, and should be chosen to tone with the material from which the house is built. Remember to see the paving both wet and dry before buying it because the colours can change dramatically.

The paving narrows to a path as it sweeps round the curve of the central bed, which is thickly planted with shrubs and small trees, and then widens again in the far right-hand corner of the garden. The view of this corner from the house is more or less obscured by the shrubs in the central bed. In this secluded corner, there is a small shell-shaped pool, mounted on the ivy-covered wall and fed by a mask water spout just above it. The spout and pool are connected by a pipe and the whole is powered by a concealed electric pump (see page 184).

The construction of this pool takes advantage of the existing brick wall; you could not satisfactorily mount a pool on a wooden fence. In a garden which is fenced all round, it is necessary to build a retaining wall for the central raised bed, and this can be extended to support the pool.

Against the end fence, in the corner to the left of the pool, there is a corkscrew hazel (*Corylus avellana* 'Contorta'). This is a slow-growing woody shrub with fascinating twisted branches. In the spring it has 'lambstail' catkins, also slightly twisted but bright enough in colour to be visible from the house, and these are followed by similarly distorted leaves. It is a very attractive oddity, a good plant to sit and look at; facing it, on the right of the pool, the retaining wall of the raised bed is thickened to form what is a resting place, if not quite a seat.

To increase the pleasure of 'discovering' this corner in the spring, the shrubs on this far side of the raised bed are underplanted with lilies of the valley, which are unseen until you walk around the curve of the bed when they can be both seen and smelled.

The garden has three trees, which is a lot in a small plot, but they are all small or easily controlled so that they can create the enclosed, forested feeling that the garden needs without taking over completely. In the raised bed and near the wall, there is *Rhus typhina*, the stag's horn sumach, which is a small tree best known for the dramatic red colour of its leaves in autumn. For autumn foliage, this is not the best site for it; it takes on the brightest colour when grown in full sun, but it does have other virtues. Its large leaves give it a very graceful arching shape in summer whereas the winter branches have a quite different, upward-reaching silhouette, looking more like a sculpture than a mere tree. It always has a rather exotic look to it which is emphasized here by setting it over attractive shrubs with glossy evergreen leaves.

In the bottom left-hand corner of the garden there is a birch tree, and there are several species that would be suitable. They are good trees in small gardens because, although they may reach 6–9m (20–30ft) in height, their slender trunks and narrow, rather open heads give them a light look that stops them from becoming over-dominant. The silver birch, *Betula pendula*, has a very graceful, attractive shape, even in winter, and acquires the bright, white bark that gives it its name as it matures. The variety 'Dalecarlica', also called the Swedish birch, tends to develop this bark a little earlier than the species. *B. papyrifera* is a species in which, as it matures, the silver bark begins to peel away in long strips, and this constant renewal gives the palest

A wall-mounted water spout in the far right corner of the Wilderness Garden.

Above: Garrya elliptica, *a hardy and fast-growing shrub which has male and female flowers on separate bushes. Here the long, trailing male catkins add colour to a garden in late winter and spring.*

Right: *Herbaceous perennials and small shrubs overflow from a brick-built raised bed.*

colour of all, often a dirty yellowish pink. All three are hardy and will tolerate most soil conditions. Other attractive birches are *B. ermanii* and *B.* 'Jacquemontii'.

Against the fence round the birch are two plants of *Garrya elliptica*, a fairly fast-growing shrub which is hardy almost everywhere, though safer in a protected corner in cold areas; it can be tied into the fence to prevent it overflowing on to the path. It has leathery evergreen leaves with a slight sheen of silvery scales which look good beside the much brighter silver colour of the birch bark.

Garrya elliptica is one of those plants that has male and female flowers on separate bushes. With most shrubs of this kind, holly and skimmia for example, the feature that is the selling point, the reason for wanting the shrub in the garden at all, is the colour of the berries. To ensure good fruiting you need to be sure to buy female plants to carry the berries and at least one male plant to fertilize them. In this garden, the long, trailing male catkins of *G. elliptica* are its greatest asset. They are silvery in colour, much lighter than its leaves, though a little darker than the bark of the birch, and they drape the branches throughout the late winter and spring. This is a case when two male plants would be ideal. The best way to sex

Senecio laxifolius, a very useful grey-leaved shrub which will grow in almost any situation, including shade, but should be pruned annually to maintain dense growth and a compact shape.

the plants is to buy them from a garden centre or nursery in early spring when the catkins are clearly identifiable.

The third tree is *Eucalyptus gunnii*. This is a very versatile species. Left to itself it is a fast-growing, fairly narrow, upright tree with a grey bark. For the first couple of years it produces juvenile leaves which are round, and pale blue-green in colour, sometimes even grey. After this the adult foliage appears and the leaves become narrower and rather darker. The juvenile foliage is the more spectacular and can be preserved by pruning. If the plant is coppiced, or cut back to a bole at ground level each year, it will grow like a shrub; it can be pollarded, by letting it grow a trunk or leg of 1.5–1.8m (5–6ft) and then cutting all the branches back to the top of this trunk. This is just the same kind of pruning that is traditionally carried out on willow to produce the young, straight, whippy growths, called withies, that are used for baskets. The final effect is of a small tree with a distinctive, round mop-head of bright, grey, juvenile foliage, but this is only maintained if the tree is pruned annually in spring. If it is neglected, the tree will quickly grow towards its natural shape and size, and will develop adult foliage.

Below the rhus and the eucalyptus, the raised bed is densely planted with shrubs, mostly evergreen, and some herbaceous perennials. There is *Choisya ternata*, which has scented white flowers and wonderfully glossy evergreen leaves. It grows so well in shade, providing the garden is not too exposed, and makes a dense, dome-shaped shrub. Any stems which shoot up longer than the others and spoil the shape can easily be cut back. In contrast with the clear green leaves and rounded shape of choisya is the architectural, grey spikiness of *Onopordum acanthium* (cotton thistle). It is a large and very prickly plant, with very pale leaves.

Most grey-leaved plants prefer the

sunshine, but onopordum will cope with some shade, as will the grey-leaved mulleins. Two shrubs which have grey leaves but which will also grow well in some shade are *Salix lanata*, which is a shrubby willow with feltlike grey leaves and fat, rather appealing catkins, and *Senecio laxifolius*. This has round grey leaves and will grow almost anywhere, but its very reliable temperament often leads to it being neglected and left to become very straggly, when it looks awful, with bare, scraggy, woody stems and a mere tuft of foliage. It needs trimming annually to keep a dense shape.

Fatsia japonica is another large-leaved shrub, which always looks slightly exotic in the garden. This will grow in dense shade, but is best in a sheltered position in very cold areas. Its flowers form creamy balls which grow up on stems above the foliage in autumn and persist through the winter. There is a bigeneric hybrid (a cross between members of two different genera) called × *Fatshedera lizei*, a cross between a variety of *F. japonica* and the Irish ivy, *Hedera helix* 'Hibernica'. It is a sprawling plant with deeply lobed leaves

Fatsia japonica, *another shrub which thrives in shade, and with its large glossy leaves gives an exotic touch to a garden.*

Contrasts in colour and leaf shape can work well using herbaceous plants in a small garden (above) *and on a larger scale using trees and shrubs* (opposite).

rather like those of its fatsia parent. This attractive climber grows best with the support of a wall or fence, but is very easy-going in other ways and thrives almost everywhere.

At the far side of the raised bed, near the pool and water spout, there are a couple of plants which grow best in a slightly damp atmosphere and moist soil, although both will grow in ordinary garden soil providing it does not get too dry. There is *Rodgersia aesculifolia*, introduced originally from China which has leaves almost exactly like those of the horse chestnut (hence its species name – the horse chestnut belongs to the genus *Aesculus*). It turns bronze in autumn once established. The other moisture-loving plant is an ornamental rhubarb, *Rheum palmatum*. It has leaves like those of the edible rhubarb, and giant heads of red or dark pink flowers.

Round the edge of the raised bed there are low-growing or trailing shrubs and plants to cover and soften the brick edging. *Viburnum davidii* will grow to about a metre (3ft) in height, but tends to sprawl, so that its dark, dull green leaves will overhang the wall. *Cotoneaster horizontalis* will do the same, although 'hang' is too gentle a word for its spiky herringbone branches; they look as though they have forced themselves down. Some herbaceous plants will soften the edges, like the big leaves of bergenia. *Bergenia cordifolia* has particularly bold leaves, and pink flowers in spring.

The emphasis in this garden is on foliage plants rather than on flowers, but there are many shade-tolerant flowers that would grow beside them and brighten the basic pattern of strong foliage shapes and colours. *Dicentra formosa* and *D. spectabilis* (both pink) would do well, as would Solomon's seal (*Polygonatum* × *hybridum*) which also has a variegated form, and false Solomon's seal which is also known as false spikenard (*Smilacina racemosa*). The smilacina is less well known but is attractive with arching stems and lightly scented early summer flowers.

The narrow bed along the left-hand fence is devoted to climbers, which will cover it as densely as possible. In particular there are several kinds of ivy. The species with the largest leaves is *Hedera colchica*, but there are also some very attractive varieties of the common ivy, *H. helix*. In dense shade, the varieties with entirely green leaves will do best, perhaps *H.h.* 'Hibernica', but where there is a little more light there are a number of variegated kinds. 'Glacier' is a fairly vigorous variety of common ivy with very subtle green, silver and white foliage. It is bright enough to lift the dark colours of the others, without looking too startling.

Evergreen honeysuckles also look good on a fence like this. They generally have less spectacular flowers than the deciduous species, but are still scented. If they are fairly thoroughly trimmed each year, they form a soft but dense mass of foliage. Close to the house there is a summer-flowering white jasmine (*Jasminum officinalis*), chosen for its vigorous growth and the way in which its branches frame the view from the window as well as for its sweetly scented summer flowers. Below this window which overlooks the garden is a small curved bed convenient for a herb garden, providing it is not shaded throughout the day. If it is, herbs can be grown in pots or in terraced beds round the shorter limb of the 'L' part of the garden.

This corner of an L-shaped garden can be a problem to cultivate. Because it is inevitably shaded for most of the day at least, the choice of plants is somewhat restricted. It is overlooked from the house through one or even two windows or doors, so that its appearance from the house is important, particularly in winter, when the rest of the garden may be too

A spring garden where climbing plants add height and variety of texture in a small enclosed area.

Hydrangea petiolarius, *a tolerant climber that will fill large areas of wall or fence even in awkward or shady corners.*

wet or cold to venture into. In addition, this may also be the area that has to house dustbins, some kind of washing line and other domestic essentials.

One solution is to cover as much of the wall as possible with some of the more tolerant climbers; *Hydrangea petiolaris* and *Jasminum nudiflorum* will grow in quite dark and unpromising corners, and the yellow flowers of jasmine will cheer any winter day. Another idea is to build a narrow raised bed which can take any of these climbers, as well as some of the more shade-tolerant herbs, such as mint and parsley, and trailing plants to fall over the edges. Pots of brightly-coloured summer bedding plants can be raised in a sunnier corner elsewhere in the garden and carried in when in flower to brighten the gloom. The raised beds cannot lessen the shade in which the plants grow, but they do improve drainage, and so increase the range of possible plants.

The other use to which this kind of structure can be put is to hide dustbins and provide a kind of outdoor cupboard that will hold garden tools, particularly for a garden like this which has no lawn, and consequently no need to find a home for probably the largest piece of equipment, the mower.

THE MANUSCRIPT GARDEN

This design is derived from gardens depicted in medieval manuscripts and is intended for a small rectangular plot. The pattern is symmetrical and formal, with carefully planned planting to soften the lines. The beds are slightly raised, and are enclosed by bricks which are also used as an edging for the gravel paths. In the centre of the garden is a small pond, and in each of the four beds round it is a crab apple, 'Red Siberian' or 'Yellow Siberian', underplanted with low-growing and shade-tolerant plants. The raised shrub beds round the boundary of the garden stand against a wooden fence topped by a trellis with arches at intervals which provide support for climbing roses, in tones of red or yellow, depending on the choice of crab apple. The marginals in the pond include rushes, arums and iris and can also be varied with the colour scheme. This design combines the variety of modern garden plants with the formal shapes of the medieval garden.

The design of this garden is derived from the illuminations which accompanied some of the medieval manuscripts. These often show gardens which are generally small and rather domestic in scale, in some ways much more like our gardens today than others that are more recent. Some of the manuscript gardens are devoted to medicinal herbs, with neat, rectangular raised beds, enclosed by a trellis fence. But beside them lie pleasure gardens, where ladies can recline round a pond or fountain.

A garden of this kind today could well be filled entirely with herbs – some culinary, the remainder chosen from those plants that were once used for food or medicine but now have a place only in the flower garden. They could even be grown one species to a bed, as the monks arranged them, presumably to avoid mistakes when gathering poisonous plants for medicines. But there is no need for the style of the garden to restrict planting in this way. It can also be planted in a contemporary way, with a mixture of small shrubs and herbaceous plants, species which were unknown and uncultivated then.

This design is for a small rectangular plot. It is symmetrical, with clear, strong lines, but the planting, particularly round the side beds, softens these lines and prevents it from looking too formal. This garden does not demand a particular style of house; it could suit a period house as well as one on a modern estate.

One difference between this garden and its inspiration is that the beds are not in line, for ease of gardening or access with a wheelbarrow, but offset, for the pleasure of a meandering pathway about the garden. From the house you can look straight down the garden, through the trees to the fountain and then on again to a seat beyond. But when you walk, you have to take a different route, with views and details to enjoy on the way.

Again, the beds are not all rectangular in shape, as they generally appear in the illuminated manuscripts, although they are, like the originals, small and slightly raised. The soil is contained by a brick edging, with matching corner stones. These corner pieces are made in several colours to match different edging materials, but can also be used to blend with brick colours. They are an important detail here and give the beds a neat and finished appearance. The paths round the garden are surfaced with firm gravel and again edged with brick. This gives a double line round the shape of each bed, which strengthens the line of the pattern they make and also prevents soil from creeping on to the gravel.

Round the boundary of the garden there is a brick-built raised bed, 30cm (12in) high and 50cm (20in) deep. The outer fence of the garden stands on this and consists of a one-metre-high (3ft) close- or feather-boarded wooden fence topped by a 50cm (20in) trellis with arches at intervals. This gives some height and privacy to the garden, and provides support for a climbing rose at each arch. The roses nearer the house should be darker in colour – perhaps 'Aloha', followed by 'Summer Wine' (both these are shades of coral pink) and then the faintly pink 'Swan Lake' at the farther end. Or the whole scheme could be darker, with a red rose, such as 'Danse du Feu' nearest the house; or in shades of yellow, with, perhaps, 'Emily Gray'. The effect of using progressively paler colours down the garden, is to make it look longer. The opposite scheme, with dark colours at the end, could be used to shorten or square off the appearance of a very long narrow plot. The arches are positioned so that they are in line with the paths across the garden; if you turn a corner towards the fence you are walking towards a rose.

In the centre of the garden there is a pond with a small, very simple fountain and in each of the four beds round it there is a flowering crab apple, *Malus* × *robusta*, 'Red Siberian'. Sometimes called the Christmas crab, this tree has vivid red fruits which remain on the tree well into the winter. 'Yellow Siberian' has similar yellow fruits which are less brilliant in appearance, but it is a good alternative if the brickwork of the house tones better with shades of yellow. The yellow fruits would look wonderfully mellow against yellow brick and would also tone with the kind of red bricks that do not go well with red fruit and flowers. Trees of either variety have a spreading, very broad shape, so that the four of them will quite soon begin to form a kind of screen through which the rest of the garden can be glimpsed.

Small symmetrical beds, edged with box and intersected by gravel paths, make a simple and elegant design which is compatable with either a modern or period house.

The central pond is round and encircled by a single row of bricks, laid on their sides, away from the pond, like rays. The pond can be constructed in several ways (see page 182), but because of its precisely symmetrical shape this is an occasion when the easiest method might be to use a moulded shape in glass fibre. There are plants growing round the edge of the pond, and these marginals need to be in shallower water than the true aquatic plants, so choose a pond mould that has two levels, making a shelf round the perimeter and about 20cm (8in) below the final water level.

On this marginal shelf there are clumps of *Iris laevigata* which has varieties in shades of blue, pink and white. With the iris there is *Butomus umbellatus*, the flowering rush, which has pink flowers in early summer and a purple tint on the young leaves, and *Acorus calamus* with its green-white flowers and sword-shaped leaves. Both these will reach 60–75cm (2–2½ft) in height. In contrast to the sharp, erect foliage of these plants, there is *Calla palustris* (the bog arum), planted as close to the edge of the pond as possible, so that its wide, dark, heart-shaped leaves spill on to the brick surround. It grows to about 15cm (6in) in height and has white flowers like those of the arum, followed by red berries.

In a garden where yellow colours predominate – if you are using yellow roses and the yellow-fruiting crab – then choose marginals such as *Scirpus zebrinus* (the zebra rush) with *Acorus calamus variegatus* and a yellow iris, such as one of the varieties of *I. pseudacorus*, or *I. laevigata variegata* (which has blue flowers but very striking variegated foliage). *Calla palustris* could again be chosen as a contrast, with its white flowers, or there are a number of yellow-flowered marginals, including *Mimulus luteus* and *Caltha spp.*, the marsh marigolds, with single or double flowers.

In the deeper part of the pond there is water hawthorn, *Aponogeton distachyos*. This has narrow oval leaves floating on the surface and white flowers which continue through most of the spring and summer. Growing beside it is *Hottonia palustris* (water violet), which has long-lasting, very pale lilac flowers, and pretty fernlike foliage.

The easiest and most satisfactory way to grow all these plants in a small pond is to plant them in plastic baskets which can be bought in various shapes and sizes from nurseries or garden centres which specialize in ponds and aquatic plants. The baskets can then be supported on bricks or blocks of some kind so that each plant is at exactly the right depth. Generally speaking, if a plant is to be grown at a particular 'planting depth', this means the depth of the water between the top of the basket and the surface. If the plants are not yet big enough to reach the surface at that depth, prop them higher until they are, and then remove this extra support as the plant grows.

In the centre of the pool is a small fountain, produced from a simple jet set at water level and powered by a submerged electric pump. This circulates the water that is in the pool; there is no water inlet. A system like this is not complicated, particularly if a power source is installed when the garden is first laid out (see page 27). The fountain adds light and movement to the water, making it more of a central focus in the garden. It also helps to oxygenate the water but it is still advisable to use some oxygenating plants. The hottonia already planted is such a plant and there are many more, most of which grow entirely submerged.

Beneath the crab apple trees in the beds which surround the pond, there is an assortment of low-growing, hummocky plants. The effect is of an irregular blanket of different shades of green, starred with flowers of every colour; the plants should be chosen from those that keep good foliage and have a bright solid clump of leaves, with small flowers and a maximum height of around 15cm (6in). This emphasis on foliage allows the use of a full range of colours without clashes. When densely flowering plants are grown, choose their neighbours with care, or interplant them with, for example, *Festuca glauca* to soften and separate the colours. There is no formal edging of plants round the beds, but plants that trail to some extent will clamber over and against the brick edging.

For spring colour, include crocus, snowdrops, aconites and 'glory of the snow' (*Chionodoxa luciliae*). The grape hyacinth *Muscari botryoides* is always

Simple symmetrical beds are softened here by herbaceous planting. This combination of pinkish flowers, edged with evergreen bergenia and in a frame of trim grass and weathered stone, is particularly attractive.

A French fifteenth-century garden from a manuscript of the Roman de la Rose. *This shows elements of design characteristic of the period, including a* potager *separated by an open-work fence from the flower-studded grass of the pleasure garden.*

reliable, either in the usual blue or the less common and less vigorous white variety. *Anemone blanda* has pretty blue flowers in spring and will cope well with shade. Many of the alpine flowers are the right size and shape for a bed like this, but they need, above everything, very well-drained soil, and most do best in sun rather than shaded by trees.

The smaller species of *Geranium* would do well, not the pot plants sold in summer as 'geraniums', which are really species of *Pelargonium*, but the true geranium which is a genus of hardy herbaceous plants with species ranging in height from a few centimetres up to a metre (3ft) or so. There are some 400 species in the genus, quite a number of which are useful garden plants, both attractive and reliable. The individual flowers are not particularly striking; they are pleasantly pretty, but no more. There are quite a lot of them, however, generally over a long flowering season. The leaves are an attractive shape, and their only disadvantage as garden plants is that they tend to straggle. If, instead of dead-heading the fading flowers, you remove the entire, long stem that carries the flower, the denser foliage which remains will continue to look good for the rest of the summer, and may even produce more flowers. These geraniums have a long history; four of them are listed by sixteenth-century herbalists. Several of the smaller species and hybrids would be suitable here, including 'Ballerina'.

Many primulas do well in partial shade, including the many varieties of *P. vulgaris*, the common primrose. The original species is argued by some to be the loveliest of all and can be grown from seed or purchased as a young plant, but must not, of course, be taken from the wild. There are many others which are suitable, such as the hybrids and varieties of *P. juliae*, which include a couple with purple leaves and paler flowers which are particularly attractive ('Guinevere'). If they flourish they spread easily, and it is the sort of plant that is often passed from one friend to another without the exact variety being established. *P. denticulata* is lovely too, with a pale rosette of leaves and straight, brave 'drumsticks' of flowers. The auriculas, varieties of *P. auricula*, were among the very first show flowers, hugely popular a hundred years or so ago but now seen much less often; they too would do well here and deserve a place in more modern gardens.

Among other suitable plants are thrift; rock rose; small species of *Sedum*; *Saponaria ocymoides*, particularly the variety 'Compacta'; species of *Prunella*, or self-heal, although this is invasive and needs to be kept within bounds; species of *Pulmonaria*, some of the less vigorous or invasive ground-cover plants (page 160); species of *Hosta*; and many more.

Slightly taller herbaceous plants grow in the three rectangular beds near the house. There is nothing very large; generally heights are in the range of 15–50cm (6–20in). For the spring there are mostly yellow flowers, with some blue, and as summer progresses the colours are bright, with yellow, white and orange, spiked with a little red.

In the matching beds farther down the garden, the flowers have softer, mistier colours, with a lot of white or grey foliage and lavender colouring. There are also a number of plants which are fragrant, by virtue of either their flowers or leaves, because these beds are near the seat.

The seat itself is a wooden bench underneath a trellis arch. Over the arch there is a highly scented climbing rose, such as 'Gloire de Dijon' or 'New Dawn'. To be truly in keeping with the medieval origins of this garden plan, no doubt the seat should be turfed, either with grass or camomile or some other creeping foliage plant that releases its scent when crushed. As a feature, a curiosity or a talking point, this would not be difficult to build, being no more than a brick or timber box with a layer of rubble for drainage, and topped up with a good topsoil which must be thoroughly pressed down and precisely levelled before being turfed or planted. It would be appropriate and atmospheric, but undoubtedly also very damp. For anyone who wants to use a seat as well as to look at it, a plain wooden bench would be more practical, as well as being in a suitable style. The bench stands in a small alcove in the raised bed that runs round the perimeter of the garden. It is backed by the outer wall and fence, with the trellis extended upwards to fit the arch.

The raised border round the garden is planted with small shrubs, larger herbaceous plants and climbers as well as the roses that cover the trellis arches. The plants are chosen for their foliage more than their flowers, so the effect is one of thick, luxuriant growth with different shades of green and a variety of shapes.

Near the house there are some of the larger herbs, such as lovage and angelica, which may both need tying in if their long stems begin to overhang the path. Here too, within easy view from the house, is the place to plant some hellebores, a lovely genus of hardy herbaceous perennials, best known for *Helleborus niger*, the Christmas rose. The lenten rose, *H. orientalis*, also flowers in late winter, lasts for weeks and flowers in all shades of cream, pink and dark purple. They are rather quiet, subtle plants, but all have good foliage, with fairly large leaves, and flowers that are a delight when not much else is about. They do best in shade.

On the sunny side of this garden is a passion flower, *Passiflora caerulea*. This is a very attractive climber which grows vigorously when conditions suit it, bearing very complex, rather exotic-looking flowers with very little colour in them. It never makes a very spectacular show, partly because of its pale colour but also because the flowers tend to come out a few at a time over several weeks, rather than in one flush. It is not very hardy, although it will often regrow after frost damage. Once it is established, it may form yellow oval fruits, but they will ripen only in an exceptionally warm summer.

Another shrub included in these beds is *Leycesteria formosa*, which has fairly large leaves on long straight stems and dark, claret-coloured flowers followed by darker berries. In colder gardens, leycesteria dies back during the winter but the stems reappear in the spring and can grow to as much as 1.8m (6ft) in a season. Because the shrub is grown in a raised bed, this means that the flowers and fruits will be arching overhead.

There is also a lacecap hydrangea, a variety called 'Whitewave'. These plants have both fertile and infertile flowers in each head, and this gives them the lacy appearance from which they take their name, in contrast to the more familiar 'mophead' group which have denser, more solid-looking flower heads. Like most hydrangeas, both these groups do best on an acid or neutral soil. Grown on chalk, they will become very slightly pink in colour, although the change is nothing like as dramatic as that which takes place in the blue varieties. An application of iron or aluminium sulphate will restore

A deep trellis arbour enclosing a seat, built on the corner where two paths intersect in the gardens at Villandry in France.

the original shade. These chemicals do not alter the pH of the soil (see page 124) but alleviate the particular problem that alkaline soils cause in hydrangeas, and will not improve the growth of other lime-haters in the same soil.

Against the fence on the shadier side of the garden is another hydrangea, the climber *H. petiolaris*. If grown on a warm wall, this will eventually cover the side of a house very handsomely, but it does seem to be able to cope with colder, shadier situations although it will not reach such a great height. It is self-clinging, with aerial roots, but in a small garden it is better tied and trained to grow along the fence. It does not need pruning to maintain flowering, but can be cut back as necessary to keep its shape. The lowest branches will also grow forward and tumble over the front wall of the raised bed, softening the look of the brick edge. *H. petiolaris* can also be used as ground cover, when the main shoots creep along the soil surface and the flowers are carried on upward-growing lateral branches.

Among the suitable herbaceous plants for this border is *Astrantia major*, which has tripartite leaves that form a particularly attractive dense clump when on moist soil. They are a very bright green when they emerge in spring, but tend to get pale and rather scruffy-looking as the soil dries in summer. The flowers are very pale in colour, with a hint of pink-green, and an unusual papery texture; they look almost dried even when the blooms are new. They come out in midsummer and last for weeks, so that both the flowers and leaves are good value in the garden although the plant dies back completely in winter. Flower arrangers love them.

On the shady side of the garden there is Solomon's seal (*Polygonatum* × *hybridum*, but sometimes called *P. multiflorum*) and a white variety of *Dicentra spectabilis*. The common name for this dicentra is 'bleeding heart', which suits the dark pink, heart-shaped flowers of the species, but seems inappropriate for this variety, 'Alba'. Both the Solomon's seal and the dicentra have arching stems with hanging white flowers. The dicentra comes out first, in spring, and is soon followed by the polygonatum. Both are beautiful and both grow well in shade, although the dicentra can also cope with a sunnier position.

Several species of *Euphorbia* can also be used. This is a genus of rather striking plants, including the familiar Christmas house plant, poinsettia. The perennial species that are generally grown in gardens usually have grey leaves and greenish yellow flowers. There are species ranging in height between *E. myrsinites* at 15cm (6in), through to *E. robbiae* at 45cm (18in), to *E. wulfenii* which will reach to more than a metre (about 4ft). They all originate from southern Europe or the Middle East and need a sheltered position. Even so, they are not reliably hardy in colder areas. They are, however, very dramatic in apperance, particularly if all three are used in one view, so that their characteristic form is echoed at different levels. In a raised bed like this, *E. myrsinites* will hang over the front wall.

In all but a chalky soil, include *Camellia japonica* for its dark, glossy, evergreen leaves and magical flowers. A variety like 'Alba simplex' would be suitable – this has white flowers and will eventually reach two metres or so in height (6–8ft), but has an upright form of growth and will not spread too far over the pathway. Camellias are surprisingly hardy, but do not cope well with sudden changes of temperature, so although they may comfortably survive a frosty night, the flowers could be damaged by early morning sun. They need to be in a position where they can warm up gradually through the morning.

There are a number of decorative grasses in this border, as there were clumps of *Festuca glauca* in the crab apple tree beds. The tallest is *Phalaris arundinacea* 'Picta' which has variegated leaves almost a metre in height (3ft), with the flower heads on taller stalks. This grass has a system of rhizomes rather like couch grass, and on moist fertile soil it should be contained in a bucket, like mint. On dry or clay soil the rhizomes do not grow very long and the clumps are easily restricted by pulling away the outside shoots. The leaves look their best in early summer but, providing they do not get too windswept, their colour remains into the autumn when they fade to a pale straw hue. *Molinia caerulea* 'Variegata' and *Helictotrichon sempervirens* are two shorter species. All three contrast well in shape with broad-leaved shrubs and plants and with darker foliage colours.

THE JAPANESE GARDEN

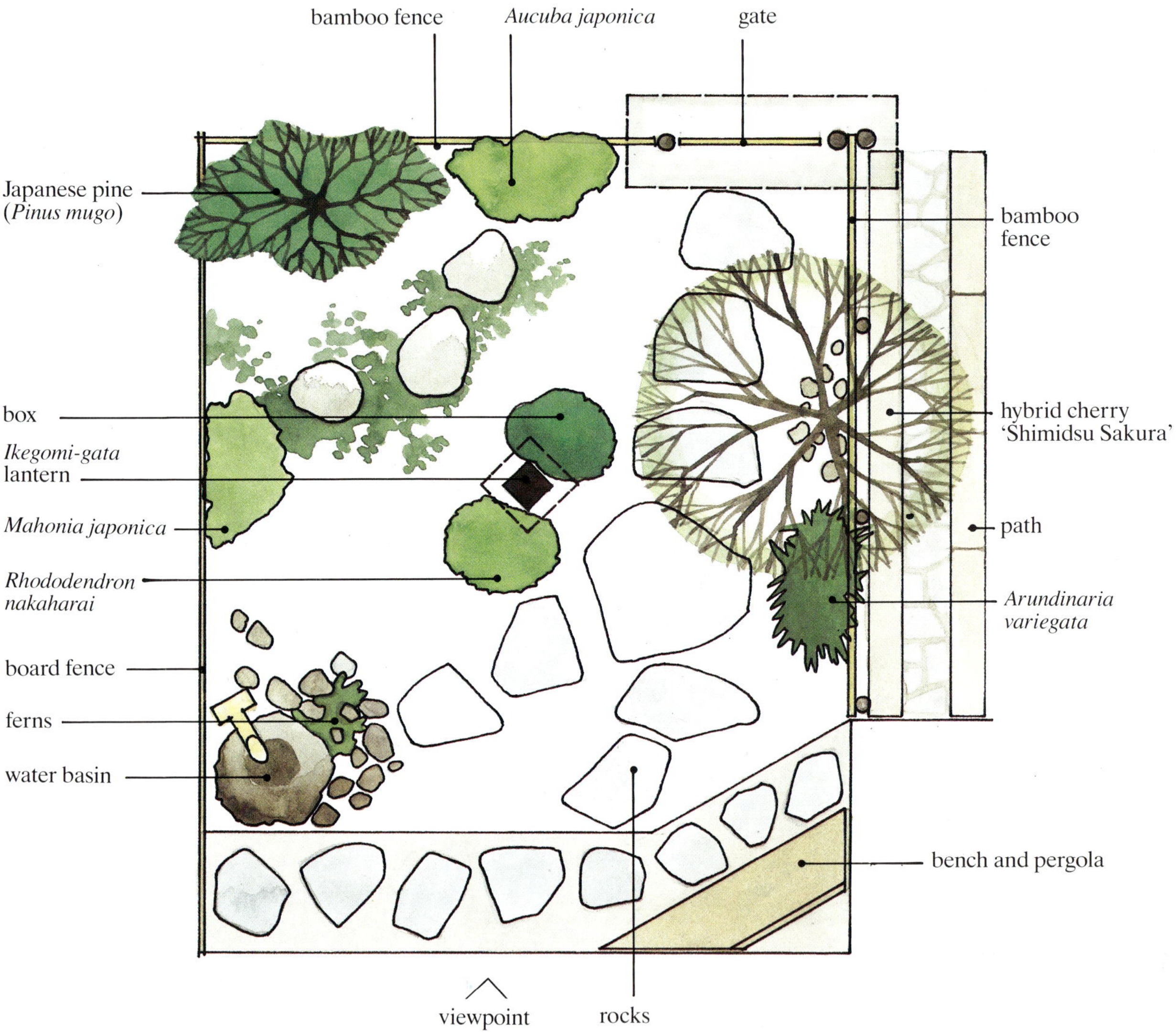

Japanese gardens have distinctive characteristics which can be used in a recognizable style. This design is likely to be a tranquil corner in a larger garden, although it could also be used to fill a tiny courtyard. There is a narrow terrace immediately outside the house, leading on to the Japanese garden itself which is enclosed by a bamboo fence. Some of the character of the garden depends on the use of naturally weathered stone and this is used in the terrace and in the garden beyond. There is a stone lantern, placed in the traditional way at an angle in the path, and this can hold a candle or bulb to light the way. Beside the house is an overflowing tsukubai, *or washing bowl, part of the essential preparation before the tea ceremony. Traditionally a ladle is always laid across the bowl so that anyone who passes may drink. The path of stepping stones leads to a gate in the bamboo fence, under an arch and into the larger garden beyond.*

Japanese gardening has a history even longer than our own, but the two traditions hardly met until the middle of the nineteenth century when Japan became more open to western visitors. The whole culture of this newly accessible country, or at least a superficial interpretation of it, became suddenly fashionable. In the years since, very many gardens that are Japanese in style or inspiration have been made in Europe and, particularly, in the United States.

It is really about as reasonable to speak of 'Japanese' gardening as a single style as it is to do the same of 'European' gardening. Over the centuries each has embraced such a range of styles and ideas that one garden could not possibly typify them. However, some approaches, derived from many different phases of the history of gardening in Japan, have transferred to the west and survived. Inevitably this adoption of some elements only in a gardening tradition has meant a loss of understanding of the philosophies from which the original designs arose, but it has left us with a mish-mash of ideas that together produce a style that we recognize as Japanese.

In a way this Japanese style is of more use in a modern garden than are many European designs. The scale is more

A late nineteenth-century painting showing the washing bowl and lantern that were a preliminary to the tea ceremony and so became traditional ornaments in a Japanese garden.

compatible, both because some of the original gardens were less grand than their European equivalents and also because the ideas within them adapt well to a small plot. Japanese gardens have clear, uncluttered, even – to our eyes – rather stylized shapes; they are ideal for a small garden and often more suitable for an urban site, surrounded by buildings, than is the relative lushness of an English country garden.

You could say of a Japanese garden, as you could of an eighteenth-century English landscaped park, that it is 'natural' in origin, but the two could hardly look less alike. The perfectly designed park should look uncontrived, as though a beautiful view existed by chance just outside the windows of the country house. The Japanese garden never imitates nature in this way; rather it stands as a symbol of the natural world, attempting to capture something of the essence or spirit of a landscape by translating it into a garden.

This is done in part by omission. When compared with an English garden, a Japanese garden looks sparse and empty, because any plant or stone or feature that is not absolutely essential is pared away until only the true core and nature of the scene remain. In contrast, other features are emphasized, particularly rocks, which are both the skeleton of the landscape and themselves capable of imparting ideas and emotions.

One of the aims of the art in Japan has been to make a place, or a picture, which is quiet and reflective, somewhere where the peace of the garden can be enjoyed as a contrast to the stress of the busy world outside.

The plants too are trained to grow in a way that exposes their true character. To western eyes the trees in a Japanese garden sometimes look almost contorted, but the aim of all this careful pruning is never to twist the tree into some alien form, but always to allow it express its essential nature.

It is not an easy style for a European gardener to encompass, accustomed as we are to filling our gardens with shapes and colours. But the strong feeling of peace and tranquillity that pervades a Japanese garden is achieved only by extreme restraint and by using empty space in the same sort of way that Japanese ink paintings use white paper.

This garden is intended to take up a small area of a larger plot, though clearly it could also fill a tiny courtyard. French doors from the house open on to the garden, which is almost square in shape and enclosed by a bamboo fence. There is a narrow terrace outside the doors, made from carefully smoothed concrete, set with a series of irregularly shaped natural slabs and edged with a line of closely placed convex coping stones. There are different textures, shapes and shades leading from the house into the garden and, to frame the view, there is a split bamboo blind over the doors instead of a curtain. Looking through the garden, past the bamboo fence and lattice gate, you can see the rest of the plot, treated in a quite different style, with grass and trees making an area for both adults and children to walk and play in, as well as a background for the Japanese garden.

Alongside the garden, linking the house to the area beyond, is a stone path. One of the keys to the characteristic use of stone in a Japanese garden is that it is placed and laid in a way that draws attention to its nature, rather than just as something flat to walk on. This path is made with several different kinds of stone, with different colours and textures, with some very large slabs interspersed with much smaller pieces. To economize, the very long rectangular slabs could be replaced by old railway sleepers, which have a texture and strength almost equal to a slab of stone. All the stone is roughly finished or, best of all, naturally eroded so that its shape, texture and patina emerge. The mixture of regular and irregular shapes within the path, like that of the terrace, makes a link between the hard angles of the house and the informal plants in the distance.

Within this garden, there are several elements that originated in the tea gardens of the sixteenth century. The tea ceremony took place in a room or building reached by walking along a path through a small garden. For purely practical reasons, since the ceremony often took place in the evening, the path was lit by a lantern, and these, usually made from stone, have remained a common feature in Japanese gardening to this day. They were made in a number of styles that have become traditional, and replicas can be bought, usually made from cast reconstituted stone.

In this garden the lantern is positioned in the traditional way, at an angle in the path, where it could usefully light the way in two directions. It is of a type called an *Ikekomi-gata* lantern, made without a pedestal, and with the shaft set directly into the ground. The advantage of this, particularly in a small garden, is that it enables you to choose its exact height, so that it balances the garden as a whole.

A modern garden which relies heavily on the lantern to give it a superficially Japanese style, not 'authentic' but nevertheless pleasing.

Plants and artefacts combine to give a Japanese effect in the English countryside.

Because it lacks a pedestal, the lantern needs to be anchored visually in some way; this is done using two shrubs, both closely clipped to slightly asymmetric shapes so that they resemble living rocks rather than plants.

This technique of close-cutting shrubs is used in many Japanese gardens, sometimes on a very large scale. The shrubs are generally evergreen, small-leaved and sometimes also flowering. Near buildings, the combination of hard shape and living plant acts as a link between the animate garden and the inanimate architecture, as in European gardens. Around the lantern in this garden, two shrubs are used. One is a low-growing azalea, such as *Rhododendron nakaharai*, which originated in Japan, and this is planted in front of the lantern column or shaft with a taller box behind.

Lanterns today can be wired for electricity and so switched on with ease. The effect of a glimmering candle, however, is much softer, and the function of a lantern like this has always been to shed a gleam of light rather than to floodlight the whole area. Panels of tracing paper set in the lamp housing will diffuse the light and obscure its source as well as protecting it from the wind.

The effect of light on stone is always most marked when the stone is wet, and many Japanese gardens, in daylight as well as after dark, look most striking when the textures of the rocks within them are emphasized by water. It is even, apparently, a Japanese custom to sprinkle the garden with water to enhance its appearance when guests are expected. In the corner of this garden, beside the house, there is a waterfall, arranged around the traditional *tsukubai*, or washing bowl, which was part of the purification associated with the ceremony of taking tea.

It is possible to use natural or carved stone in making one of these basins. Sometimes they are of a curved shape, in contrast to natural rocks about them,

sometimes carved in some detail. Natural stones that have had a wide hole cut in the top to hold a post or pillar in some building are sometimes reused as basin stones. In this case, the bowl is a natural rock, standing 70–80cm (28–32in) high with a shallow depression in the top. Water trickles from a pipe into the bowl which overflows so that water cascades over and down the stone, also moistening the smaller rocks and pebbles around it. Hydraulically, this is very similar to a fountain in a pond and is powered by an electric pump in the same way. The 'pond' is filled with loosely packed stones, however, so that there is no surface of water seen, only wet stone. The amount of water that circulates is clearly going to be critical, and an arrangement like this will need topping up in dry weather and may overflow in heavy rain, although this should increase the effect rather than cause any problem.

The pipe which feeds the basin should be of bamboo, fixed to the upright feed pipe with a wooden joint, and although a pipe made from a plant stem may seem unnatural to a European gardener it is not particularly difficult to construct and is cheap enough to replace when it looks too weathered. Traditionally, a wooden ladle lies across the basin so that anyone who passes may drink.

The third element of garden design that was made important by the tea ceremony and persists as a characteristic of Japanese gardens today was the use of stepping stones to make a path. When they were introduced, these stones protected the plants from the feet of visitors and the clothes of the visitors from the mud of an unmade path. In this garden, the paths really do demand natural stone and would be entirely spoiled if they were constructed from concrete slabs. Only one really large stone slab is essential; this is the irregular stone that acts as a central pivot to the paths leading to the house, the water basin and the gate, and in a way as a focus for the whole garden.

Part of the Ryoan-ji dry landscape near Kyoto in Japan. It is composed of fifteen rocks, set in five groups on a bed of raked quartz fragments. The arrangement of the rocks is widely interpreted and esoteric, but intended to link the onlooker with abstract nature.

A natural composition of rocks and water in the garden of Seto in Japan.

Stones used in Japanese gardens always look like enormous rocks, submerged in the ground so that one flat surface is exposed to step on. They never have the relatively flimsy appearance of our thin flags, with the thickness of the stone showing as a vertical surface, and so, if you use thin slabs, disguise them by chipping at their edges to make a sloping surface than looks like part of a much larger rock.

Rocks of several different kinds and colours have been used in this garden, with the contrasts of texture of granite, slate and sandstones. The long rectangular slabs can, as in the path beside the garden, be replaced by old railway sleepers. Several of the large 'slabs' are made from small pieces of stone set into mortar. Plan a slab like this in advance, composing the small rocks to your satisfaction well before mixing the mortar, so that the end result does not in any way resemble crazy paving. The small stones should not fit closely like a jigsaw, but lie together to make an attractively textured rock. Emphasize the texture by scraping away some of the mortar between the stones.

Around the paths there is a 'sea' of white granite chips, about 0.5–1cm in diameter (around $\frac{1}{4}$in), which is rather finer than conventional gravel but coarser than grit. The fact that the paving slabs are stepping stones is emphasized by setting them a couple of centimetres higher than the surrounding chippings.

In fifteenth-century Japan, the contemplative philosophy of Zen inspired a new trend in garden-making using sand and rocks as symbols not only of physical objects, like land and sea, but also of man's progress through life and towards Nirvana. Very few of the original gardens remain, the most famous example being the Ryoan-ji to the north of Kyoto, but the style is often borrowed in modern gardens, with varying degrees of success. The stone used at the time was generally the granular quartz crystals that are produced when granite rots or breaks down. They are gritty in texture and fine enough to be mounded into shapes or raked into lines and patterns.

In this garden, the granite chips are slightly larger and not laid to the kind of depth that would be necessary for raking patterns. This is, in part, because the use

Below: *Rocks, a bamboo fence and a small bridge arching over a dry river of flattened pebbles; all features that are seen individually in Japanese gardens and here combined into one small plot.*

Opposite: *A wooden bridge made in a series of segments forces a change of direction and leads the eye to different views of the garden.*

of *kare-sansui*, or dry-stone gardening, demands space and domination of the garden before its atmosphere of serious and peaceful contemplation can emerge. This is not to say that any dry-stone garden must be large; the Ryoan-ji garden is a little over 250 square metres (900sq ft) which is smaller than many suburban plots, but it does mean that you cannot expect the full effect of the style to appear in competition with too many other features and ideas.

The chippings are edged with larger, flattish stones and behind that there are plants, shrubs and a couple of trees. It is not necessary when making a garden with a Japanese style to be entirely committed to species that originated in Japan, although it is not difficult to do so because the rich flora of that country has helped to fill our gardens with its exports since the eighteenth century. It would be much harder to make any garden without including natives of Japan.

In the far left corner of the garden, looking from the house, there is a gnarled, shrubby pine, *Pinus mugo*. In this small area of the garden, the aim is to grow a small number of plants and with them achieve a feeling of woodland trees. In composing a conventional shrubbery, evergreens are used as blocks of solid colour and are pruned to encourage dense, uniform growth. In this case, the plants are pruned in the opposite way, to open them out, exposing their trunks and limbs to become part of the picture, rather than merely to be an invisible support for the foliage.

The ground rises slightly into the corner where the pine is growing and there are three large stones around its base. They are arranged in a triangular form so that their heights increase the impression of raised ground around the tree and lead the eye down to the gate below. The setting of stones so that they look balanced and natural is a Japanese art, but the crux of it is that the boulders must be well submerged so that they look

completely stable and almost as if they have grown from the ground. Around the base of rocks it is often the custom to grow moss, but this is not always easy to establish or maintain without constant watering. Other ground-clinging plants, such as *Soleirolia soleirolii*, would fulfil the same function.

Between the tree and the gate there is a shrub, *Aucuba japonica*. This is the ubiquitous spotted laurel, beloved of Victorians and generally rather out of favour today, but with some of its branches completely cut out so that the form of its growth, the colour and exact shape of the leaves and the angle at which they hang are clarified, it is transformed and is a typical Japanese garden subject.

Almost any shrub could be similarly pruned to show its own form and character, rather than used as a blob of colour in the gardener's palette. Two others which work well are *Fatsia japonica*, which was introduced from Japan about 150 years ago and *Mahonia japonica*, which actually came from China. The other tree in the garden is a hybrid cherry, 'Shimidsu Sakura', which has graceful, rather long-stalked pinkish white flowers in spring and a distinctive, flat-topped structure.

Small plants around the garden could include clumps of dwarf bamboo, such as *Arundinaria variegata* (kept rigorously thinned), species of *Hosta*, which are enormously popular in Japan, and ferns. A sparsely growing rush might do well near the water basin, where the soil will be moist and may also encourage moss. *Scirpus tabernaemontanus* 'Zebrinus' has cream and green stripes which would echo the colour of the bamboo. Any very graceful herbaceous plant is worth considering, no matter what its origin, and some of these can be brought in growing in containers to give some variation as the seasons progress. Solomon's seal (*Polygonatum* × *hybridum*) would be a good choice, as would *Dicentra spectabilis*, which does come from Japan.

Some change with the seasons is important, and one of the advantages of having a Japanese garden as part of a larger plot is the space outside in which to cultivate pots of flowers that can be brought in for a short while when they are at their best. Chrysanthemums (the Japanese national flower) are a common choice. It is vital, however, to remember that colour in a Japanese garden is used for occasional punctuation and no more. One flower draws attention to itself by its brilliance and to its surroundings by its contrast. A row of flowers looks like a European bedding scheme.

Diagonally opposite the pine, in the corner made by the walls of the house, there is a bench seat and above it a light wooden pergola, made from triangular section wooden slats set into the wall, with the widest side uppermost. The line of this pergola follows the curve of a typical Japanese roof. It is linked to the ground by two straight wooden pillars which, like the bench itself, have square pedestals which give a weighty base and a feeling of stability which echoes the setting of the rocks and is one of the keys to the atmosphere of the garden.

The shape of this pergola is repeated in the arch over the lattice gate that leads to the rest of the garden. This gate, like the fence itself, is made from bamboo, lashed into a lattice, which is a relatively simple job, but slow and repetitive. A similar though inevitably less striking effect can be created by using other kinds of wood. The fence is light in weight and must be attached to the usual wooden posts, sunk well into the ground.

THE LIME TREE GARDEN

This is a simple, formal design ideally suited to a small, upward-sloping town garden. The plot is terraced on two levels; the lower level nearer the house is paved and steps lead from this to the finely gravelled higher level. Set into the gravel are two very simple knots, edged with a low box hedge and planted with a selection of culinary herbs, with a ball-shaped standard bay tree at the centre of each. At the end of the garden, set against the wall, is a row of lime trees, pleached in the traditional way. The trees are underplanted with drifts of small spring bulbs in a bed separated from the gravel of the upper terrace by a line of cast clay 'rope' edging. The upper terrace is retained by a brick wall and above this there is a lavender hedge. On the paved lower terrace are terracotta pots planted with a variety of climbers, cool-coloured summer flowers and foliage plants.

This is a simple and rather formal garden, which uses small regular beds similar to those seen in the gardens of medieval monasteries, or in herb gardens and the walled kitchen gardens of great houses. It captures something of the calm, measured atmosphere felt in such places but without any feeling of anachronism. It is full of soft grey foliage. There are not many flowers, and those that do grow here are either white or in shades of blue and purple, making it a cool and restful place. The house is Victorian, in a typical urban terrace. It is quite small and has the back kitchen extension which is usual in such houses, making an L-shaped plot that, in this case, slopes up away from the house towards the wall at the end.

This sloping plot has been terraced into two levels, breaking the garden into two quite distinct areas: the lower level, close to the house, is paved and four steps lead from this to the higher level, which is finely gravelled with two square herb beds or miniature knots.

The most striking feature of the higher terrace, indeed of the whole garden, is a row of pleached lime trees along the end wall. The word 'pleaching' means interweaving branches and is a technique which has been practised in some way or other for at least a thousand years. Interwoven branches form a dense thicket; pleached shrubs were used to make an impenetrable hedge for enclosing livestock, an early ancestor of the 'cut and laid' hedge still used in some places today. By Elizabethan times pleaching had moved from the farm and into the garden; Shakespeare uses the term:

> Bid her steale into the pleached
> bower,
> Where honeysuckles ripened by
> the sunne
> Forbid the sunne to enter.

In more recent times, pleaching in the garden generally applies to trees. It is a technique that can be used to very good effect, sometimes to delineate a walk or alley, and sometimes to make a barrier which nonetheless allows a view through, between the trunks, and in an odd way makes the prospect beyond even more inviting.

In this modern garden the trees are clearly not planted to enhance the view because they actually stand at the end of the garden, only a metre or so from the boundary wall. They make a strongly shaped endpiece, high and sheltering, but with a lightness and interest that could not be produced by any conventional hedge or line of trees.

Lime and hornbeam are the trees traditionally used for pleaching, although in principle almost any tree would be suitable. Of the two, the lime is perhaps the more attractive, with heart-shaped leaves that have a wonderfully brilliant pale colour in the spring. The lime is also called the linden tree, and acclaimed for its scent, but this cannot be relied upon once the trees are pleached, because it is the flowers that provide the perfume, and there will be fewer of these after pruning. The common lime throws suckers at the base of the trunk, making a tuft of new green growth that some people find ugly around any tree. Certainly it would mar the effect of a line of pleached trees. In addition, the leaves are very prone to attack by aphids which deposit a sticky honeydew which eventually drips from the trees and is only too familiar to car owners who park under them in city streets. There are, however, a number of

The tradition of 'pleaching' trees is very old. Here the branches are intertwined, pruned and trained on wires to give a stilt-like effect.

A traditional herb garden, with different species separated by box hedging, but also planted with some herbaceous flowers.

hybrids, like *Tilia* × *euchlora*, which are immune to aphids, and it is worth checking on them first with the nursery which supplies the trees.

Use three-year-old trees to start the pleaching and choose standards, that is trees which have been grown so that they have 1.6–2m (5½–6½ft) of bare trunk before the branches begin. Sink absolutely rigid poles, one on either side of the garden, and at intervals of 2m (6½ft) between. Across them, stretch wires 30cm (1ft) apart 1.8–3m (6–10ft) high. Plant and stake the young trees in the usual way. In the autumn remove the leader shoot of each tree at a height of about 2.5m (8ft) and look carefully at the direction of growth of the remaining branches. Tie to the wires any branches that are growing in the right directions, that is to say more or less parallel to the line of the trees. Cut back the remaining branches, those that are growing too far out from the line of trees to be trained back in. As usual, cut back to a bud, but check that the bud is growing away from the centre of the tree from which it grows, to encourage the trees to grow out towards each other and to prevent ugly crossed branches. Limes are not difficult to manage and take well to heavy pruning.

The bed the limes grow in is separated from the gravel which covers the rest of the upper terrace by a dark-coloured, cast-clay 'rope' edging. This gives the bed a neat and appropriate finish and prevents the soil and gravel from mixing and blurring at its edge. The trees are underplanted with purple and white crocuses. Like most flowers, these look better when planted in fairly big blocks of a single colour, and not mixed together. They would be best in clusters of, say, 60cm (2ft) across, but not in rigid lines or symmetrical patterns. They should provide apparently natural drifts of brilliant spring colour.

The gravel on the upper level should be fine in texture, grey rather than yellow in colour, and properly bedded and rolled so that it is firm to stand on. A lot of garden gravelling is all too reminiscent of a walk across a pebbly beach.

The two small knots or herb beds are very simple in design, with nothing of the intricacy that developed during the sixteenth and seventeenth centuries. They are each surrounded by a box hedge, about 30cm (1ft) in height. Box, *Buxus sempervirens*, is a beautiful evergreen shrub that has been used in a dwarf form, like the variety 'Suffructicosa', to edge a bed in this way for hundreds of years. It is

Above: *A classic knot, reconstructed in a London garden.*

Right: *A simple knot, with a brick surround, centred on a sundial. The warm colour of the bricks and the soft purple and grey tones of the herbs and flowers are in sharp contrast with the brightness of the sundial's white pedestal and the grass beyond.*

rather out of favour these days because it is slow-growing, but even this has its brighter side; the more slowly a hedge grows, the less often it needs clipping to maintain its shape. Set the young box plants 20–25cms (8–10ins) apart and cut back the leading shoot to encourage them to bush out. They look attractive almost immediately and fill out to a dense hedge within a few years.

There is another small-leaved shrub that is sometimes recommended as an alternative to box, called *Lonicera nitida*, which is a relation of the honeysuckle although to the untutored eye it is really nothing like the familiar scented climber. It does grow faster than box, and is also evergreen, but it lacks the wonderful texture. In a box hedge the light reflects differently from the backs and fronts of the slightly curved leaves so that the strong dark colour also has lightness and variation. A box hedge is worth waiting for. An alternative would be the grey-leaved *Santolina chamaecyparissus* which is a small shrub with compact yellow flowers. It is easy to prune into a low

hedge and looks very striking, although the pruning prevents flowering.

In the centre of each knot there is a standard bay tree, with a ball-shaped head above a bare stem, about 1m (3ft 3in) high. Sweet bay, *Laurus nobilis*, is Mediterranean in origin, and, although an evergreen, it is hardy only in sunnier areas, or if grown in a very sheltered spot. But in this garden it would be quite easy to keep two standard bays in terracotta pots, about 35cm (14in) across, which could stand in the centre of each knot for most of the year, but be moved to somewhere more sheltered in the worst of winter. In the biting North American winters it is common to see evergreens bundled in sacking to protect them from frost damage. As much as anything, these blankets prevent the shrubs from losing water through their leaves which they cannot replace through their roots because the soil is frozen. It makes an odd sight, a garden apparently scattered with tightly bound hessian packages, but it does enable the gardeners of New England to grow all kinds of evergreens that otherwise would not stand a chance through the winter.

Very many of the herbs that we grow for the kitchen came originally from warmer parts of southern Europe and need planting with a little care if they are to do well. They can stand a certain amount of frost, but hate above all to be in cold, damp, or worse still, waterlogged soil through the winter. If the garden soil is heavy and full of clay, it is very important to lighten it with organic matter, like peat or compost, and even to dig in some sand or grit before beginning the knot beds.

Round the bay tree the knot is divided into four equal beds by a cross of bricks. There are four herbs planted in the garden, two in each knot, with two little beds of each kind, planted opposite each other. In this case the herbs are chosen because their colours and textures complement each other, but others could just as well be grown. In a household where herbs are important for cooking, four different herbs could be grown in each knot. If one of them is mint, plant it in a submerged box of some kind, something like a bucket with the bottom knocked out, or the underground rhizomes will spread right through the knot and probably up into the gravel as well. Mint is a notoriously invasive plant and thoroughly deserves its reputation. There is more about herbs and herb gardens on page 147.

The strong line of the lime trees at the end of the garden is repeated in the lavender hedge which tops the retaining wall at the front of the upper terrace. Although lavender would never make the kind of barrier that keeps animals in or out, it does make an excellent low hedge. In summer, when it flowers, it looks and smells wonderful, but the foliage keeps its grey colour and some of its perfume throughout the year, so that the hedge is never entirely without interest. Because the effect of the hedge is greatest when it is thick and dense, start with strong plants about 30cm (1ft) apart. They will join up in a couple of years, but if they are neglected once they reach full size they will soon become very woody and gnarled, with stems like an old tree trunk carrying a sparse fringe of foliage and flowers. Once they get like this they are hard to rejuvenate because they do not respond well to cutting back into old wood. It is much better to keep them green and vigorous with regular annual pruning.

The time of year for the main pruning is spring, when the plants should be trimmed with shears 2–3cms (1in) or so into the previous year's growth. This stimulates the new growth that will carry the flowering spikes. A further trim after

Detail of the brickwork within the simple knot in the Lime Tree Garden.

A lavender hedge lining a pathway in an English country garden.

flowering keeps the plants dense and tidy, but any autumn growth will be vulnerable to frost damage, so in colder areas the plants are better left untouched until the spring. The varieties 'Hidcote' and 'Munstead Dwarf' are more compact than the species.

In the past, lavender flowers were made into oils and tinctures to cure a variety of ills, as well as perfumes to mask the smells of a less well-washed age. The Romans apparently used lavender in their bath water, hence its name from the Latin word, *lavare*, to wash. Any flowers picked for drying (and from a dense lavender hedge you can cut plenty without even seeing the difference) should be picked before the tiny blue flowers that make up the spike actually open. Their scent is greatest if they are picked in the morning, before the sun gets too hot, and dried in the shade.

The lower terrace is paved with rectangular stone slabs and the plants around it are grown in an assortment of terracotta pots. Almost any plant can be grown in a pot, but they do need much more careful and regular feeding than they would in garden soil and are very dependent on watering during the summer. On the steps between the two terraces, there are pots planted with blue pansies and *Stachys lanata*, which is also sometimes called lamb's lugs or pig's ear. This is a plant generally grown for its foliage, which is densely covered with hairs, giving it the appearance of silvery grey fur. It is pretty to look at and compelling to touch but its great popularity lies in the way that it frames and enhances the appearance of other, more brightly coloured flowers. It is often seen at the front of mixed and herbaceous borders and its spreading growth also makes it suitable for ground cover on a fairly sunny, well-drained site. Grown in a pot it sprawls over the edge and gives a silver frame to the other plants in the container. It is a perennial but needs a sheltered site in the winter and, for this reason, is sometimes grown as an annual.

The tall chimney pots which frame the steps are planted with the lesser periwinkle, *Vinca minor*. This is an easily

Below: *Carefully shaped, low box hedging, set in brick paving, marks the division between herbs and flowering plants. The pattern in which the bricks are laid is changed in the path between the hedges.*

Opposite: *A knot garden made from box with gravel around and within. The contrast of the white-painted seat highlights its design.*

grown perennial mostly used as an evergreen ground-cover plant because its long trailing stems root at every node or leaf joint, which makes it spread very quickly. Those same trailing stems will cascade elegantly from a tall pot, staying green throughout the year but starred with flowers in the late spring. When you see *V. minor* grown in gardens it almost always seems to be the original blue species. But in fact there are several varieties with white, purple, burgundy and even double flowers, which are just as vigorous in their growth as the species. A combination of white (the variety 'Alba'), blue (the species) and purple ('Atropurpurea'), all trailing from a pot, is beautiful.

There are trios of pots at each corner on the lower terrace, raised on bricks or blocks at three levels. The lowest pot is the same as those on the steps, planted with stachys and pansies. The next has a purple sage (*Salvia officinalis* 'Purpurascens'), and the highest has a tricolour sage (*S. o.* 'Tricolor'). Both these are surrounded by a white campanula, such as *C. carpatica* 'White Star', which overflows the pots and cascades down the sides. The leaves and flowers of these plants follow the grey and blue colour plan, with the two coloured sages adding to the texture.

Left: *A corner of the Lime Tree Garden.*

Below left: Jasminum officinalis, *a vigorous, white-flowered climber popular for its scent which is strongest at dusk.*

The terrace is surrounded by three walls: two belonging to the house which opens on to this garden, and the third from the house next door. These three walls are covered with white-flowered summer jasmine, *Jasminum officinalis*, growing in large pots. This is a lovely climber for a garden that is used for sitting in, particularly in the evening, because it has a wonderful scent which is strongest at dusk. It is a twining climber which needs some kind of rigid net or trellis to support it. This should be fixed firmly, but there must be sufficient gap between the wall and the trellis to allow the stems of the jasmine to grow through. New growth arches away from the support which gives the plant an attractive depth and shows off the flowers, but if it gets too unruly these long stems can easily be tied back. Summer-flowering jasmine grows vigorously and makes an effective arbour in a very few years.

There is another climbing plant in the corner between the wall of the house and the left-hand garden fence. This is *Clematis alpina*, sometimes more dramatically labelled the 'Alpine virgin's bower'. It has fairly small, blue flowers and rather attractive foliage, but like most clematis the plant is deciduous. There is an evergreen, *C. armandii*, which has beautiful, glossy, green leaves and would also be ideal for this corner, but it will grow only on a sheltered wall with a sunny aspect. *C. alpina* is much hardier and will grow particularly well in a cool, sheltered corner. Both of these are species, rather than hybrids, and do not need any pruning unless they get out of shape.

One of the virtues of this garden is that although it requires a certain amount of effort to set up, with earth-moving and wall-building needed to construct the terraces, it is not a difficult or time-consuming garden to maintain once established. The pleached trees and the box hedges need attention occasionally, and the only part of the garden which needs watching day by day is the pots. They will dry out in any but the wettest summer and the plants in them will also need regular feeding if they are to do well.

THE ELEMENTS OF A GARDEN

Gardens are made by combining and interweaving elements and features according to a plan or design. The gardens in the last section showed eight particular combinations, stimulated by the ideas and philosophies used by gardeners in the past, but the possibilities are infinite; all or any of these features, and others, can be put together in a way that suits your taste, ability, pocket, imagination and the space and site available. So this section is about the 'ingredients' – the elements that can be used to realize your garden – and about their practical difficulties and limitations as well as their origins, their points of interest and their attractions.

SOIL

The soil is the most basic raw material in your garden. Every garden dream you ever have depends on it and the best-realized garden dreams are those that are tailored to fit the soil available. But having said what sounds depressingly like a word of warning, it is also true that every soil can be improved and, however unpromising it looks at first, can grow a good garden if you understand it and exploit it.

Cutting down into the earth, the first layer you find is the topsoil, and in gardening terms this is usually what is meant by 'soil'. Then there are various layers of subsoil and below that the bedrock, where you leave the world of horticulture and enter geology. From the point of view of the plants, the important bit is the topsoil. If the subsoil is very compacted, it may prevent the topsoil from draining, but deep or double digging will improve this. Otherwise, the only direct contact you will have with the subsoil is if you need to move it in order to create a change of level in the garden.

As its name indicates, the topsoil needs to be on the surface. Before making a terrace, building a bank, or doing any kind of earth-moving, it is very important to remove the topsoil and put it safely to one side so that it can be replaced, on top, when the excavations are complete. If you are having a house built it is also worth making sure that the builder is setting aside the topsoil when he digs the foundations, or you may need a second mortgage to buy topsoil for the garden.

Topsoil is made up of two parts. The first is organic, called 'humus', and is

The crisp clean colours of spring bedding, but calcifuges like wallflowers will not thrive in acid soil.

derived largely from rotting vegetation and the corpses of the hosts of tiny organisms that live and die in the soil. It is consumed by more of these same organisms which excrete it in the form of soluble nutrients, the most natural fertilizer of them all. In an undisturbed plant community, where nothing is picked and nothing taken away, the humus is constantly renewed by falling leaves, dying flowers and so on. In the artificially tidy environment of a garden, the humus content needs topping up with annual additions of compost, manure, peat, etc.

The inorganic part of the soil is made from ground-up fragments of rock. These may come from the bedrock below but in some parts of the world they are likely to have been carried from elsewhere by glaciers, thousands of years ago. As the glaciers advanced, they gouged and tore at the rocks beneath them, creating a massive mixture of rock and rubble that they carried with them as they crept

A collection of heathers, characteristic of gardening on acid soil. There are varieties of heather in flower in every month of the year.

across the country. When the ice melted, this debris was left behind and it is gardened on today.

The texture of the soil in your garden depends largely on the size of the particles of this ground-up rock. If most of them are large, the soil is sandy (sometimes also called a light soil); it will be easy to dig and will drain well, indeed sometimes too well, because the water that percolates through it so easily is carrying soluble nutrients out of the reach of the plants that need them. In a dry summer, its inability to hold water will demand a great deal of irrigation.

If most of the particles are very small, you have a clay soil. It will be heavy to dig and in the worse cases will drain so badly that surface water collects on it in puddles every time it rains. It is probably the hardest and most depressing kind of soil to begin with, both for the gardener and the plants. It is sticky to touch, very difficult to break up with a fork and correspondingly hard for roots to force their way through.

Somewhere between a clay soil and a sandy soil there is the soil that all gardeners would like – a good loam. This has small, medium and large soil particles in such a balance that it has the advantages of both clay and sand but the problems of neither. It is not found as often as one might hope.

On a sandy soil, because the addition of humus helps to retain water and valuable soil nutrients the best treatment is to dig in quantities of compost or manure. If both are unobtainable in the centre of a town, use peat from the garden centre and cultivate the habit of buying a bag of manure or the sweeter-smelling, spent mushroom compost on every country visit, although peat and mushroom compost do not contain nutrients.

Surprising though it seems, the same remedy is generally also the key to improving a clay soil, even though its characteristics and problems are the exact opposite. Humus helps to break down the electrostatic charges that 'stick' the tiny clay particles together, making them aggregate or 'clump' together which lets the air in and improves the soil texture. Gypsum (calcium sulphate) and lime have a similar but less lasting effect. Frost is another weapon which attacks this clay bonding – the traditional practice of autumn digging helps to increase the surface area exposed to the winter weather. When faced by a neglected garden on heavy clay soil, cling to the thought that although it may be dreadful now, clay has great potential. It can be lightened, and, when it has been, it will still retain water and nutrients and so make a very good garden soil. But it will take time.

Acid and alkaline soils

If soil is derived from an alkaline bedrock such as limestone, it will be slightly alkaline. Soil formed over hard igneous rocks tends to be acidic. Acidity and alkalinity are measured on a pH scale, which runs from 0 (strongly acidic) to 14 (strongly alkaline). The pH of your soil can be measured fairly accurately using a kit which can be bought from a garden centre. It may make the whole affair sound alarmingly scientific, but if the soil in your region is at either of the extremes it will restrict the number of plants that can be grown on it to the extent that you can probably find out what type it is by walking round and seeing what other people are growing successfully.

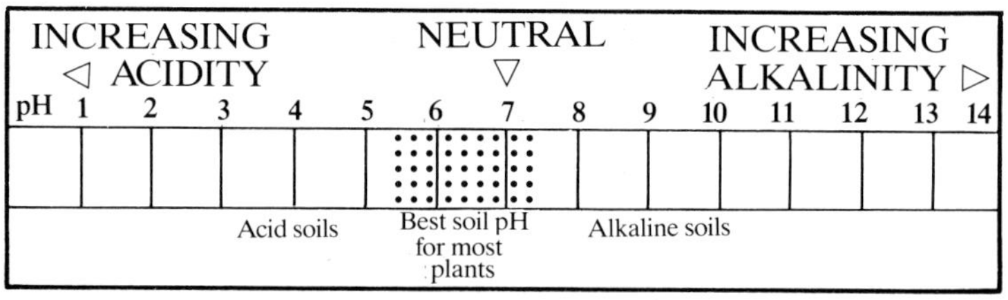

The pH scale. All soils occupy a small fairly central band of the entire scale, which runs from 0–14.

Some plants, called calcifuges or lime-haters, will grow only in a neutral to acid soil. So, if your neighbour has a garden in which rhododendron, camellia, azalea and heather abound, then you can safely assume that the soil is acid. On the other hand, if these shrubs are found only in pots, then it is likely that your soil is alkaline (sometimes referred to as limy or chalky). The opposite of calcifuge is calcicole. Some alpines are calcicoles, as are most of the enormous cabbage family, which includes wallflowers as well as the familiar vegetables.

Hydrangeas will grow in either acid or alkaline soil but their flowers change colour according to the soil type; they turn pink in acid soil and blue in alkaline. One of the effects of acid soil is that certain minerals are tied up chemically and made unavailable to the plant, even though there may be ample in the soil, and it is this that causes hydrangeas to behave just like the litmus paper in a pH test, with flowers that are pink or blue, depending on acidity. It is quite interesting to know what the pH of your soil is, but it becomes a problem only in extreme cases. If you do decide to measure the pH of your soil, take several readings round the garden to avoid freak variations.

If you want to alter the pH of your soil, it is easier to make it more alkaline by adding lime, than it is to make it more acid. Slightly acid soils are sometimes the result of poor drainage, so the problem may be solved when the garden is better cultivated. The only way to grow the real lime-haters on chalky soil is by isolating them, either in pots or by digging a hole and lining it with polythene, perforated for drainage, and filling this with a suitable soil. Acid compost is sometimes marketed as 'ericaceous', that is, suitable for the acid-loving genus *Erica*, the heathers.

On the whole it is better to adapt your ambitions to the garden rather than embark on a long battle with the environment, because it is easier, but also because plants blend into their surroundings and often look wrong when persuaded to grow in what is really the wrong place. It is better to enjoy a healthy tree peony, growing well on alkaline soil, than to struggle with a magnolia that will never do really well.

PLANT NAMES AND CLASSIFICATION

Many gardeners are put off by the Latin names which are attached to plants. They seem hard to pronounce, difficult to remember and impossible to spell. In fact they have a very clear purpose, custom and use soon simplify them, and it is genuinely worth sorting out what they mean and how they work. What they actually do is give to every plant a unique name, one which is valid throughout the world and can be understood by any and every botanist, naturalist or gardener whatever their native tongue. With this name a plant can be identified precisely and the confusion that comes from common names is avoided.

The proper name of a plant also gives some indication of its pedigree and its close relations. All plants are classified according to some or all of their similarities and differences. The plant kingdom is divided into classes – flowering plants, cone-bearing plants, etc. The flowering plants are divided into subclasses, each of which contains a number of orders. Each order is made up of families, each family of genera and each genus of species. Rather than recite a complete and tedious pedigree every time a plant needs naming, it is generally identified by the name of the genus and species to which it belongs. Both parts of this binomial, as it is called, are printed in italics. The name of the genus, which is sometimes likened to the plant's surname, always has an initial capital whereas the name of the species does not.

A species is sometimes further divided into varieties. If the variety occurs in nature, its name just follows after the name of the species in italics. If the variety is a cultivated one, and in gardening that is often the case, then the name is again written after the species, but in Roman rather than italic type, with a capital initial letter and within single inverted commas.

When two species of the same genus are crossed, the resulting plant will have an × before its species name to show this. Less commonly, crosses between members of different genera have an × before their genus name.

The name of the genus alone is often used as a kind of shorthand. Where there is only one species in the genus or one species is cultivated much more than any other, this is accurate enough for most uses, although it can sometimes cause confusion.

CHOOSING AND BUYING PLANTS

Most garden plants are bought from garden centres, nurseries or a variety of non-specialist retail outlets and markets. Each of these has some advantages and disadvantages.

Plants sent from nurseries, by post or some other carrier, are generally 'bare-rooted', that is, they have been grown in open ground and dug up for sale. They will be sent at the right time of year, generally autumn or spring, and will need immediate attention. If their roots are allowed to dry out, they will be permanently damaged, so they should be planted immediately or, if this is impossible, given a temporary home by heeling them into a trench elsewhere in the garden. Sometimes the root ball and the soil it holds are wrapped in sacking before despatch, and this wrapping should be removed just as the plant goes in, so that the roots are not allowed to dry. These wrapped plants transplant better than those with bare roots.

Plants bought from garden centres are usually 'container grown', that is, they have been grown in some kind of pot or container for some time. In some cases the containers are conventional plastic pots; in others they are no more than little bags made from polythene or treated paper with holes in the bottom. Plants can be left in these containers for a while after purchase if it is not convenient to plant them, but will need watering regularly. Container-grown plants should have a good root system which, ideally, fills the pot more or less exactly. If you lift a container-grown plant gently by its stem the whole pot of soil should come with it. If the soil falls away, the roots are not established. The containers are sometimes embedded in peat or gravel when

A good local garden centre will sell a fairly wide range of container-grown plants. With some care, these can be planted at any time of the year and the selection offered should give some idea of which species are hardy in the area.

the plants are displayed for sale, and the roots grow out of the pot and into this medium. In this case you will have to cut the container away before planting, and will be lucky to manage this without damaging the roots.

Shrubs and trees are best planted when they are dormant, that is from autumn to early spring, providing the soil is not actually waterlogged or frozen solid. The main advantage of containers is that they extend this season so that planting can take place at any time of year, but on a sunny site and in hot weather it is still very important that the plant gets enough water, and the best way to do this is to 'puddle' it in, by filling the hole you dig for it with water. Continue to water regularly while the weather remains dry.

Garden centres can be very attractive places; you can walk round them and actually see what you are getting before you buy it, and if you need extra information and help, there should be somebody about to answer your questions. Garden centres also give you a fair idea of what plants are hardy in your part of the country.

It is not always extremes of temperature which do the damage, but the length of the growing season – that is, the number of days in the year in which the daily temperature is high enough to allow growth. It is possible to divide the world into climatic zones in which certain, more tender, plants will or will not grow, but in practice, the microclimate of a garden, particularly in a town, may vary substantially from the average for the area. Take local advice and, when you choose a plant which may be vulnerable, balance this against its importance in your design or just how much you love it and want it in your garden.

On the other hand, the selection in a garden centre is fairly limited. A general nursery will stock a selection at least as wide, and there are many specialist growers who have a much wider choice of particular ranges of plants. Most nurseries can be visited if you are close enough; some operate by mail order only. It is, however, certainly possible to stock your garden entirely from a good-sized garden centre; many of the popular plants they sell became so popular just because of those horticultural virtues you are seeking. But at some time you will almost certainly want or need a wider choice, or you will want to buy more specialized plants (such as ferns or alpines), or to have a better selection of varieties of plants such as roses and clematis. Then you need to buy from specialists, many of which advertise in gardening magazines and newspapers. If you have any query or problem, write to the nursery; most are pleased to help.

There is not a lot to be said in favour of buying from greengrocers or DIY shops or the host of other places which sometimes keep a few plants in addition to the normal stock of their trade. You may be lucky and find a bargain, but you are more likely to be disappointed.

TREES AND SHRUBS

If there are trees and shrubs already established in your garden, take a look at their age and general condition. On the whole, if there are decent-sized trees in a garden it is worth thinking very carefully before chopping them down just because they are not compatible with your plans for a new garden design. Although not sacred, fifty years or so of growth should not be wasted lightly and mature trees add valuable character to a garden. On the other hand, there are people who have planned their garden round an existing tree, only to find later that it is fundamentally unsound and falls down in the first winter squall or needs felling for reasons of safety. If in doubt take advice from a tree specialist, which in some areas is possible through the local authority. Trees which grow very close to the house may also be damaging the foundations and need to be removed.

When you mark a tree on the garden plan, record not only the position of its trunk, but also the area that is overhung by its branches. You can assume that the roots of the trees will affect the soil for roughly that area, and this will undoubtedly restrict the plants which can be grown there. Not only will the ground be shaded from light by the branches, but the tree's efficient and established root system will absorb most of the available water and nutrients, leaving the soil impoverished and inclined to dry out in summer. There are many plants which do well in shade, where the soil is sheltered from the sun and generally moister than the rest of the garden, but few can cope with the poor, dry shade immediately under a large tree. When nurseries and garden centres label a plant with details of the conditions in which it will grow, this is a distinction that they sometimes fail to make. If you are enquiring about the suitability of a particular plant for growing in a shady area, it is important to specify whether the shade is that of a building or a tree.

Trees and shrubs are the largest and most architectural elements in a garden design. They are also the slowest to mature and the hardest to move once established. Clearly they are important. They should not be planted without considering their nature and attributes, their exact siting and the role they will play in the final effect. Many people hesitate to plant a tree at all because they fear that it will take too long to reach a size that is interesting. In fact there are plenty of species that grow quickly, provided that they are fed and cared for, and one or two, such as the blue gum (*Eucalyptus gunnii*) and some of the conifers, whose growth is very fast.

Trees and shrubs are often considered quite separately, as two different subjects. In fact, a tree is a plant which has a single woody stem or trunk whereas a shrub, although it also makes woody growth, has a number of stems, but the distinction between a large shrub and a small tree is often unclear and there are some species which can be persuaded to grow into either form. In a small garden, the two have so many roles and functions in common that they can be considered together.

One of the major functions of trees and shrubs is to enclose a garden, providing seclusion and some degree of privacy. The distinction between seclusion and privacy is an interesting one to ponder when planning the garden; total privacy can really be achieved only by erecting an

The shape of the mature tree is an important part of its character. Weeping species are invariably described as such but densely leaved and open-branched trees also each create a completely different effect which is often not evident in a young plant.

oppressively high, completely solid hedge, wall or fence – and even that will allow the penetration of sound. A feeling of seclusion, on the other hand, can be created with a much lighter barrier, making the garden feel enclosed without entirely overshadowing it. An open centre with encircling trees and shrubs can create a secure oasis, quite apart from the environment outside.

Trees and shrubs are also used to separate and define different parts of the garden, either for visual effect or to distinguish areas that are used in varying ways – for sitting, or playing, and so on. They can also obscure an ugly building. When siting a tree or shrub for this purpose, remember that it often works more effectively if the plants used are close to the point of view rather than on the edge of the garden close to the offending object. This is partly a matter of perspective: an object close to the eye obscures more than the same object farther away. But, more than that, something placed close to the observer also seems to hold the eye and so make everything beyond recede into the distance. In this way, the impact of a large, ugly building can be lessened, even if it is too big to be completely obscured.

Trees also give scale to a garden. If everything in a small garden is in miniature, it makes the plot seem smaller still. A tiny garden cannot be filled with forest trees, but planting trees and shrubs of reasonable size as part of a garden design does not make the area seem cramped; it gives an agreeable feeling of being a secluded part of a larger whole.

A tree can also give shade in a sunny garden, either the heavy shade of a dense evergreen, or the lighter, dappled shade of, say, a fruit tree or a maple. When positioning a tree for shade, bear in mind the way in which the shadow moves through the day and how this changes with the seasons.

The choice of trees and shrubs available today is enormous, much larger than

Clipped bays make a strong shape that stands out against an informal background of trees and shrubs.

The pleasure of this garden owes as much to the variety of shade and texture in the leaves as it does to the colour of its flowers. The bright leaves of the catalpa catch the sun in contrast with the softer colours of the blue cedar and weeping willow.

that seen by our ancestors. For example, in northern Europe the last ice age wiped out all but the hardiest species, so that when gardening began the choice must have been fairly limited. As their empire stretched across Europe, the Romans spread, too, a few home comforts, including the sweet chestnut tree, the mulberry and the medlar. Centuries passed, bringing the discovery of the New World, increasing exploration in Asia and a flood of new species. Many of them must have proved a disappointment, being too tender for their new environments, but many survived and tree-collecting became a gentleman's pursuit. The 'arboreta' that resulted were generally for botanical interest and to test the hardiness and viability of the new species, rather than for any aesthetic virtue. Some critics of garden designs today argue that this collecting mentality spread into the garden and that we are not rid of it yet.

Certainly, when selecting trees and shrubs for a small garden it is easy to be so impressed by the range of choice that you take one of almost everything and end up with a garden that is a shapeless mish-mash, lacking form and unity. A more effective composition is usually made from a more restrained number of species, by repeating colours and shapes or by

Winter colour from evergreens and the coloured bark of species of Cornus.

using species that are similar in shape or in leaf form.

When choosing trees and shrubs, it is important to consider the size of the mature specimen and not be led into planting enormous trees in unsuitable places. It is also important to consider the overall shape that the species will take, because different shapes have different uses and create varying atmospheres. For example, a weeping tree is graceful and is easy to visualize in a garden that has a feeling of magic and romance. It can also be used effectively to echo the shape or angle of a slope, or it can be used to make an arbour or shelter round a seat.

There are many more trees with a weeping habit than are commonly seen. The willow is the best known by far, in spite of the fact that it is really too big for a small garden and tends to damage drains and foundations with its roots. There is also a weeping birch, an ash and a beech. The willow-leaved pear (*Pyrus salicifolia* 'Pendula') is a very pretty, small tree which, although not as spectacularly trailing as the willow, has an overall weeping shape. Its soft grey foliage and generally tolerant disposition make it a popular choice and very suitable for a small plot.

Most weeping varieties are mutations of the original species. Some of them, like the popular weeping willow, *Salix* × *chrysocoma*, grow naturally as trees. Others, like the cherry, have mutated to produce a form with sprawling branches which would normally grow as a shrub. Nurserymen produce trees by grafting the weeping branches on to an upright trunk or stem of the original, or a closely related species. The pussy willow, *S. caprea*, can be treated the same way, as can many varieties of rose. It is important, when selecting a plant which has been grown in this way, to choose one which has an even crown, with branches all the way round.

For a stronger, more forceful profile, choose an upright, columnar tree, a shape that is also called fastigiate. Whatever their size – from knee-high dwarf conifers to towering Lombardy poplars – these trees provide a punctuation and strong contrast with the broader, softer outlines around them. Using their tall shapes to emphasize the effect of perspective can also increase the apparent length of a garden.

Where there is water, reflections become important. A fastigiate tree can provide a variation in silhouette that makes a reflection come alive, while the reflection itself doubles the impact of the shape of the tree. In a limited space, these narrow, columnar trees are also useful. For example, there is a variety of Japanese cherry, 'Amanogawa', that can be 5–6m (16–20ft) tall but only a couple of handspans wide. Although the foliage is not dense enough to make a very strong impact, the tree has a mass of lightly scented flowers in the spring, providing a splash of colour in a space too small to hold a rounder tree.

A bench of this type, built around a tree, can provide a pleasant shady place to sit, but is most successful on a paved base.

There are other trees which, although not narrow enough to be described as fastigiate, are nevertheless more upright and less round-headed than other varieties. For example, the crab apple 'John Downie' has branches that grow towards the vertical, and the result of this is a generally erect tree with a much narrower overall shape than other varieties of crab. This kind of detail of description is very often omitted from catalogues but is of great practical importance as well as making a lot of difference to the final effect of a plant in the garden. If possible, it is worth looking at a mature specimen before buying, or asking the nursery for a more precise description of a tree's mature shape.

To earn its keep in a small garden it is often said that a shrub or tree must show to advantage in more than one season. With some species, the advantages or disadvantages can be fairly easily recognized; an ornamental, flowering cherry, for example, is spectacular in the spring, but has rather dull-looking leaves throughout the rest of the summer, and bare, not particularly distinguished branches in the winter. By comparison, a crab apple has flowers in spring, and shows bright fruit that can be cooked or admired right into the autumn. Other trees earn their keep with brilliant autumn foliage or with less obvious attributes, such as attractive bark or branches that make a striking silhouette even without their leaves. Before choosing trees and shrubs it is important to assess their virtues and defects in some detail.

A shrub can be evergreen or deciduous, and the advantage of an evergreen is that it will continue to hold the outline of the garden through the winter in a way that deciduous shrubs generally cannot. In a small garden evergreen shrubs that continue to cover a fence throughout the year are valuable: species of *Cotoneaster*, *Pyracantha* and *Ceanothus*, for example. Some evergreens, such as yew and privet, which are most often seen in hedges, are even more attractive when treated

Narrow conifers used as evergreen punctuation in a mixed border designed by Gertrude Jekyll.

as shrubs. There are shrubs with dull-green leaves, including some species of *Viburnum* and rhododendrons, whereas others, such as the many varieties of holly, Mexican orange blossom (*Choisya ternata*) and camellias (where there is shelter), and laurels such as *Prunus lusitanica*, catch the light to provide a contrasting gleam.

Some conifers are the towering giants of the plant world and have no place in a small garden, but there are literally hundreds of varieties which are either small or so slow-growing that they can be regarded as dwarf trees and may remain in pots for twenty or thirty years. The other virtue of these conifers is that many of them have blue-grey or golden foliage, and the spring colour of tiny new shoots emerging against the darker background of branches that have survived the winter, is beautiful.

Deciduous trees and shrubs sometimes compensate for losing their foliage by the spectacular colour of the leaves before they fall, or by their interesting bark. Some decorative bark is brightly coloured, such as that of the very popular dogwood (*Cornus alba*). It has young growth with red bark, and annual spring pruning produces a cluster of shoots which are brightly coloured the following winter. The most striking way of growing a shrub like this is with several plants together, and at a distance from the usual point of view. The effect is then of a brilliant haze, and is much more dramatic than seems possible when examining

Blending tones in the ivy and conifers combine to soften the rather severe shape of the house.

individual shoots more closely. The larger *C. stolonifera* has yellow-green stems which contrast well with the red when there is space for a large enough stand of the shrubs.

Some rose species have decorative bark or thorns, such as *R. omeiensis pteracantha* for example. A number of trees, such as the plane trees, the birches and some of the maples, have bark which peels away, making an attractive texture and a contrast in colour with the new bark beneath. A particularly good example, which also has attractive foliage, changing colour in spring and autumn, is the paper-bark maple (*Acer griseum*).

In evergreen or deciduous species, the foliage colour can be green (either dark or

light), or tending towards blue, yellow or bronze. The leaves may be single-colour or variegated. They may look paler because they are covered in tiny hairs, or darker because they have a waxy shine. In deciduous species, the leaf colour may vary with the season, changing to a brilliant display of yellow, orange or scarlet in autumn. A more subtle beauty may result from the pale highlights of new spring growth and the daily changing colours of emerging leaves.

Each species of shrub has a potential size that it is likely to reach as it matures over a number of years, but it will also have a characteristic final shape. It may be upright or sprawling, it may grow into a near sphere with a neat outline, or it may have strong spiky branches making an irregular silhouette. The shape to which the shrub will grow may be modified by being near a wall, exposed to wind, and so on.

Some trees, and even more shrubs, have conspicuous flowers and are chosen for this reason, particularly those which manage to flower in the winter months when the garden easily looks rather bleak and spring seems a long way away. Some, such as wintersweet (*Chimonanthus praecox*), *Viburnum* × *bodnantense*, witch hazel (*Hamamelis mollis*) and winter-flowering jasmine (*Jasminum nudiflorum*) flower, as the jasmine's botanical name suggests, on bare branches, before the spring foliage opens. Others, such as *Viburnum tinus* and species of *Mahonia*, are evergreen.

For the warmer months, it is possible to choose flowering shrubs of almost every size, shape and colour. One effective way of using them is with one plant close to the point of view, with the colour echoed farther down the garden by another plant of the same species or another species with a good colour match. So the climber *Jasminum stephanense*, which has festoons of pink flowers with a slightly mauve tinge, is echoed by *Kolkwitzia amabilis* or by the darker colour of foxgloves. Another good pair is the perennial *Rodgersia aesculifolia*, which has spikes of creamy white flowers, which are repeated both in colour and texture by the prolific flowers of pyracantha. There are many shrubs with white or whitish flowers, but the similarity of the texture of these two makes them particularly compatible.

The foliage of a plant will also give it a texture that may be an important and distinctive part of its appearance. This is harder to define and describe than the colour of leaves and flowers, but just as important in arranging and juxtaposing different species. Plants with small leaves have a dense, close texture, whereas those with larger leaves generally have a softer, more open look. Curved leaves give a texture that is different from that of straight leaves, and leaves that are a markedly different colour on the upper and lower surface give another effect again. In addition, some shrubs grow in a way that gives them a texture quite divorced from their overall outline shape. A common example perhaps illustrates this best: rosemary, which is a popular herb but also quite a successful, moderately hardy, ornamental shrub, can be pruned after flowering and cut to shape; left alone, it often grows into a wide, sprawling bush, but each individual shoot grows straight up, so that the texture of the plant, seen from a distance, is of dense, vertical stripes, strong and distinctive but quite in contrast with its wide, horizontal outline.

The complexity of the characteristics of individual plants, once you begin to look at them in detail and from season to season, is somehow always surprisingly great. There are no hard and fast rules about which plants will go with which, but seeing a mature specimen before making any final decisions remains the best way of keeping the choice of trees and shrubs within the area of design rather than gambling.

ROSES

The rose family has a great history, excellent use and versatility in the garden, as well as a strange emotional importance to the world at large. Over and over again the rose has been taken as a symbol: it has been adopted as the badge of families, causes and political parties from the Middle Ages until today; it has inspired poets and painters. In the thirteenth-century French epic *Le Roman de la Rose*, the rose stood for success in life and love, and modern metaphors such as 'everything coming up roses' and 'roses all the way' continue the age-old idea that roses are something special. The metaphoric 'bed of roses', which life is not, is said to refer to the luxury of Sybaris, where mattresses were stuffed with rose petals to scent the sleepers' dreams.

In Europe there is a small number of native rose species; by medieval times,

The formal rose garden in the eighteenth-century park at Nuneham Courtney in Oxfordshire.

several more had been introduced from the Mediterranean and the Middle East. But the beginning of the explosion of varieties that exist today is much more recent, dating only from the beginning of the nineteenth century, following the import of new roses from China. These introduced one in particular startling new characteristic – repeat flowering. Until then, European roses flowered once in a season, so this ability to produce a second flush of flowers later in the season was a revolution. The new introductions were crossed with enthusiasm, the numbers of roses offered for sale increased dramatically and rose-breeding as we know it today was born.

The complexity of rose-breeding over the last couple of hundred years has produced a family tree to rival any monarchy and left us, as gardeners, an inheritance of varieties and types that can fill any niche or adapt to any style of garden. The choice of colour, of course, is enormous but more than that, the shape, form and mode of growth ensure that while there is a rose that is perfect for the softly rambling cottage garden, there is another just as suitable for the measured formality of another style. Which is just as well, since the rose is probably the single type of plant that most people beginning a garden are sure they want to include.

Formal rose gardens became popular during the nineteenth century as the new varieties became available. Hybrid tea, floribunda and standards are the ideal types for this style, and they are sometimes known as 'bedding roses', which gives a clue to the way in which they are used. It is a style of gardening that can look stunning, even in a small plot. The only problem is that bedding roses are hard, bare and thorny throughout the winter and early spring. In a larger garden the solution is simple; you walk another way and do not look at the rose garden out of season. In a small garden the winter view cannot be escaped so easily and it is worth underplanting the rose beds. Small spring bulbs are attractive – crocus and squills perhaps, followed by forget-me-nots or *Pulmonaria angustifolia*. Daffodils are less successful because their leaves look bedraggled after flowering if there are no other plants to hide them. Smaller, neater bulbs, such as the low-growing species of tulips, are more suitable. Once the roses are in full flower, underplanting is less important, but an edging around each bed hides the woody framework of the bushes. Plants with a fairly neutral colour look best – perhaps *Santolina chamaecyparissus*, dwarf lavender, hostas, or herbs such as sage, marjoram or rue.

An arch smothered with the climbing rose 'Seagull'.

In a large formal rose garden, individual varieties occupy separate beds and there is little doubt that bedding roses massed in single colours in this way are most effective. In a small garden this may be harder to achieve. Nevertheless, a small number of varieties grown in groups will almost always look more striking than a large range of varieties containing only one representative of each, even though it may make the initial choice a harder task.

Another way of extending the area of

colour of roses in a small garden is to vary the height (there is an example in the garden on page 54). In a formal garden use standard roses at the back of a rose border or in the middle of an island bed. All the bedding roses you may buy are produced by budding, that is by grafting a bud of a particular named variety on to a strong and healthy rootstock. Many varieties are budded on to a number of different stocks and can be bought as bushes and as standards, so that exactly the same flower can be grown in a different way and at different heights. The height of a standard rose depends on the stock used, and may vary from one grower to the next. Generally speaking, standard means a height of 90–120cm (3–4ft), whereas half standards will be 75–80cm (2ft 6in–2ft 8in) high and miniature standards about 45cm (1ft 6in). Weeping standards may be as tall as 165cm (5ft 6in).

All these bedding roses need fairly careful pruning at least once a year. Some gardeners prune once only, generally in spring, just before the new growth starts. Others cut the stems back by about one third in autumn, which keeps the plants tidy and lessens the chance of damaging the roots as the bushes are swayed by the winter winds. In addition, roses like these are prone to various pests and fungal diseases and may need treating at intervals through the flowering season. Whether and how often you need to spray your roses depends on the area, the weather and on the degree of perfection of bloom at which you aim, as well as on your own feelings about balancing this perfection against the use of chemicals in the garden. The tradition of growing roses without any underplanting is explained, at least in part, by the need to get at them in order to give them regular care and attention.

A manuscript painting showing a rose-covered trellis as a background to a fifteenth-century love story.

Hybrid tea and floribunda roses are now more correctly called large-flowered and cluster-flowered bushes respectively. These new names and classifications have been internationally agreed but are still not consistently used, which is a pity in a way, because they actually describe the plants. The old names are a pleasant reminder of how our roses were bred, but tell you nothing about how they grow and what kind of flowers you might expect.

Climbers and ramblers provide real height in the garden. In fact, no rose really 'climbs' at all. They have no tendrils or clinging roots, no ability to twine or twist around a support. They just put out long thorn-bearing stems which catch on any support they encounter, and either grow upwards or cascade down as circumstances determine. The labels 'climber' and 'rambler' are often used interchangeably but ramblers tend to grow new shoots from the base rather than from a framework of older wood, to be larger and more vigorous than most climbers and to flower only once. Many varieties are very old and have been grown for several hundred years. Climbers are sometimes recurrent flowering; some are 'sports' or chance mutations of bush roses, and these, like the floribunda and hybrid teas, will flower twice.

Although a second crop of flowers is a great advantage, and rose breeders have devoted many years to achieving it, some of the ramblers will always figure on any list of best-loved roses because their one flowering is so dazzlingly beautiful. They flower profusely, with each long, arching stem carrying a shower of blossom. In addition, they are invaluable as a cover-

La Roseraie de l'Ĥay les Roses is a stunning example of formal bedding roses at their most spectacular, with pillars, arches, bushes and standards in glorious flower.

ing for an ugly shed, or to climb through a tree or to reach the eaves of the house; there is something very appealing about being able to pick a bunch of roses from the bedroom window, and a rambler can provide this luxury.

Species and shrub roses are large, informally shaped bushes, ideal as part of a mixed bed or a cottage garden. Most of them flower once only, but many of the species make up for this by bearing coloured hips in the autumn. Many of them grow to a size that is too great for a small garden, but there are plenty that do not, both from the old European species and the more recent imports from China and Japan. They give nothing like the dense display of bedding roses, but often have prettier foliage, sometimes strikingly attractive bark or thorns and usually autumn hips. They are a valuable addition to a shrub border or as a background to a mixed or herbaceous border. The only pruning they must have is the attention that you would give to any shrub, namely the removal of any dead branches or very spindly growth.

The same is true of shrub roses, both the older varieties from the last century and the modern ones bred today. On the whole they become fairly big plants, but, like the species roses, they are very successful in mixed borders. Many of the old shrub roses have a soft romantic look and scent that has never been equalled; they are currently enjoying a well-earned revival of popularity.

At quite the other end of the time scale, one new type that looks set for a useful and popular future is the ground-cover rose. As the name implies, these varieties are low-growing and spread to form a mat dense enough to exclude weeds. They cope with some shade and are an attractive, low-maintenance cover that will also carry flowers for most of the summer. They can also be walked over without damage – or at least without damage to the rose; hosiery is another matter.

Like so many plants today, roses can be bought in pots from the garden centre in almost any month of the year. The way to take best advantage of the enormous numbers of varieties available, however, is to buy them from a specialist nursery, where they are generally available only from autumn through until early spring; this is the time when the plants are dormant and should be planted. When choosing varieties, it is often useful to visit shows, rose fields or gardens in the summer to see for yourself exactly what the plants can look like.

FLOWERING PLANTS

As soon as you move into a house and take over the garden, the position of the trees and shrubs is obvious. The same is not true, however, for any herbaceous plants and bulbs, and here the need to curb impatience is clearest. Try to wait for a whole year before doing anything too drastic, to make sure that you have seen everything that is already planted in the garden. During this time, cut any grass there is, weed any flower beds, observe closely what comes up where and mark it on the plan. The key is to remove only those plants that you can identify reliably, either as weeds or in some other way undesirable, and leave for further examination anything unrecognized. And do not cultivate deeply or you may accidentally dig up a brilliant and well-established display of spring bulbs that would take years to replace.

Herbaceous plants are those which retain their soft green stems and, unlike shrubby plants, do not make woody branches. They include perennials, which die back at the end of each flowering season and then sprout up again the next spring, as well as annuals and biennials. Annuals are plants which germinate from seed, grow, flower, make their own seeds and die, all in the course of one season. They are planted afresh each spring. Biennials, as their name suggests, take two years for the same sequence to take place, growing into a leafy plant the first season and flowering the next. What this means, of course, is that biennials also need sowing each year for a display of flowers each year, which is why the two groups are generally described together.

These terms were coined by gardeners rather than botanists, and describe the average behaviour of certain plants when grown in temperate climates. Quite a few annuals and biennials are actually perennial in their kinder, native climate. Others, like foxgloves and forget-me-nots which are really biennial, seed so freely that they appear each spring without being resown, and are often thought of as perennials.

Annuals are described as either hardy, in which case they can be sown directly into the garden in early spring and will survive any frost they may experience, or half-hardy, when they will not. Hardy annuals include the flowers of childhood and of romance, remembered from a cottage garden – flowers like nasturtiums

COMPILING AND

A bed or border of flowering plants very often needs to include plants that are of a variety of heights, to give it a good shape and to show the flowers to their best advantage. In addition, it is desirable, except in certain special cases, to have plants in flower for as much of the year as possible. As you go ahead with planning the border and choosing its inhabitants, you can make sure that these two criteria are fulfilled by compiling a grid or plant chart.

Use one axis for the seasons of the year and the other for the height of the plant. Rule lines to make this into a grid and you can see that there is a box for each combination of size and season. As you choose plants for the border, fill them in on the grid and it is then easy to see where there are spaces, whether there will be no height in the spring, or a flush of summer flowers followed by a barren autumn, and so on. This kind of diagram is never going to be able to create the perfect border on its own. It takes no account of colour or size of flowers, for example, or of the breadth and texture of foliage, and all these are important in deciding exactly how to place plants. But it does provide an easy way of checking some of the most vital aspects of the flower bed as you go along.

To plan a bed for a particular purpose, for example a border of herbaceous perennials, a white bed, a scented bed or one on acid soil, include only appropriate plants on the grid. To give a more accurate plan or, perhaps, a greater emphasis to a particular time of year, divide the months into five or six seasons instead of the conventional four. Used and adapted in this way, a very simple chart can be a powerful and flexible tool in garden planning.

As an example, this grid is of mixed flowering herbaceous plants, including annuals, perennials and bulbs, which would be suitable for a cottage garden. It could be used in the cottage garden on page 30, but it could also be a basis for an informal planting in many other contexts. In addition, any of the plants on the grid can be used in a host of other ways.

USING A PLANT CHART

	SPRING	EARLY SUMMER	LATER SUMMER	AUTUMN/ WINTER
TALL more than 60cm (2ft) Can also include climbers.	Honesty (*Lunaria annua*)	Hollyhock **C** Foxglove **C** Delphinium *Lavatera trimestris* **C** Larkspur (*Consolida ajacis*) *Gypsophila paniculata* *Campanula medium*	Sunflowers *Anemone japonica* (also called *Anemone* × *hybrida*) Red-hot-pokers **C** Evening primrose *Verbascum* spp.	Michaelmas daisies *Chrysanthemum* spp. *Solidago* × *hybrida*
MEDIUM 30–60cm (1–2ft)	Daffodils Tulips *Doronicum* spp.	*Aquilegia* Lupins Peonies *Hesparis matronalis* *Trollius* × *hybridus* *Stachys macrantha* *Papaver* spp. *Gypsophila elegans* **C** Love-in-a-mist (*Nigella damascena*) Stocks (*Matthiola* spp.)	*Achillea ptarmica* *Coreopsis verticillata* *Phlox* spp. Fever few *Geranium* spp. *Campanula* spp. *Chelone obliqua* Cornflower (*Centaurea cyanus*) *Centaurea imperialis* *Antirrhinum* *Nicotiana alata*	*Physalis franchetti* *Crocosmia* × *crocosmiiflora* *Helleborus orientalis*
SHORT 15–30cm (6–12in)	*Adonis vernalis* *Alyssum saxatile* Bluebells Lily of the valley Forget-me-not (a biennial, but seeds freely)	*Bellis* spp. London pride Candytuft (*Iberis umbellata*) **C** *Lychnis viscaria*	*Campanula carpatica* *Calendula officinalis* **C** *Verbena* hybrids *Convolvulus tricolor* Nasturtiums (*Tropaeolum majus*) *Reseda odorata*	*Iris stylosa* Christmas rose (*Helleborus niger*)
GROUND HUGGING less than 15cm (6in)	Pansies and hearts-ease **C** Violets Snowdrops Crocus Aconites *Aubrieta*	*Dianthus* spp. **C** *Mesembryanthemum criniflorum* **C** *Lobelia erinus* *Arabis alpina* *Saxifraga* spp.	*Limnanthes douglasii* *Sedum spurium* Creeping thyme *Geranium* spp., including *G. subcaulescens*	*Colchicum* spp. Winter-flowering Viola *Hepatica nobilis* **C**

C after a plant indicates that it continues to flower into the next season on the grid.

and marigolds, larkspur and love-in-a-mist. They can be very simply grown by scattering them on to the garden but, for the most brilliant display, it is best to keep in mind a few facts about the way they grow and how this can best be promoted.

Before sowing, prepare the soil thoroughly and rake or rub it into a fine tilth. If it is very poor, rake in a general-purpose fertilizer a few weeks before planting. Sow the seeds thinly; if they are cramped together as they germinate they will be tall and weak from the beginning. The young plants may also need thinning out as they grow. Annuals have to cram a lot of growth into a very short time and it is important that they are encouraged to become compact, bushy plants right from the start.

One of the problems which can slow or even prevent germination is that the layer of fine particles of soil sprinkled to cover the seeds solidifies to form a hard cap. Clay soil and heavy watering after sowing increase the likelihood of this happening. When the seeds germinate they hit their heads against the solid layer and are unable to penetrate it to reach the light

Above: *In a single-colour herbaceous border the colour of foliage remains an important element in plant choice and design. In this case, the leaves of purple sage are a foil for the perfect brilliance of* Verbena *'Blaze Scarlet'.*

Opposite: *An unusual arrangement of summer bedding plants with salvias, cleome and pink ageratum set within a border of grey foliage.*

and air. They contort with continuing growth and eventually die. To prevent this, water the ground thoroughly before the seeds are scattered rather than afterwards. A finely raked clay soil will harden even under rain, so cover the seeds with a sprinkling of compost or peat and sand rather than with soil.

One of the great virtues of annuals is that they are relatively very cheap and so give an opportunity to try new ideas and colour combinations, to develop and consolidate your plans and inspirations without spending a fortune. Using annuals also gives a certain flexibility to a mixed bed – shrubs and perennials go on from year to year, more or less unchanging, but a complete transformation can be achieved by altering the annual planting. In a very new garden annuals are almost an essential because they can be used to fill any gaps until shrubs and perennials fulfil their potential and take over. Sow the seeds in fan shapes or in irregular patches to that the different species are seen as intermingling clumps, at least 60cm (2ft) across.

Half-hardy annuals can also be sown directly, but only when all possibility of frost has passed, and this leaves a very short growing season. The more usual alternative is to sow them under cover and then transplant or 'bed out' the young plants when the weather is warmer.

Bedding or change-bedding is a form of temporary planting for display which can be used to fill a garden with colour and interest at every season. Plants of all kinds can be used, but half-hardy annuals remain the most popular. A number of species are generally used in a clear pattern or scheme in which their shapes and colours complement each other or, particularly, contrast with each other. It can be enormously effective. Because rearing half-hardy annuals is relatively laborious, involving sowing, pricking out and then planting on the young seedlings, and because it requires either a greenhouse or, at the very least, a decent length of well-lit window sill, many people buy them as young plants, generally called 'bedding plants' after the way in which they are most often used. But bedding demands, even in a small area, at least tens, sometimes hundreds, of plants of a single colour, and commercial bedding plants on this scale are enormously expensive. Seed merchants offer a cheaper method as well as an infinitely wider range of plants and a larger choice of single colours. As bedding has declined in fashion, more and more shops only stock bedding plants in mixed colours. Even seeds are becoming more difficult to buy in single-colour packets, although seed catalogues remain a better bet than garden centres.

Some of the bedding schemes for great houses in the nineteenth century were breathtakingly complex, and even the villas of the new industrial middle classes were surrounded by gardens that were impressively patterned and ornate. Today we lean, perhaps, more towards the informal style that followed, led by Robinson, Jekyll and their associates, while formal bedding has become a characteristic of public parks. The use of bedding that remains in domestic gardens is rarely anything but banal, which is a pity, because a small, careful bedding scheme, especially using dark and subtle colours, is a world away from clichèd stripes of white alyssum, blue lobelia and red begonia.

Bulbs, which are often the mainstay of spring bedding schemes, are favourites throughout the garden. The bulb itself is made of swollen scales, in structure rather like a leaf bud, and it stores food through a dormant period which is then used to fuel the growth of flowers and leaves. Other storage organs, like corms and tubers, have a different structure but the same function, and the term 'bulbs', or 'bulbous plants', is often used to describe them all. The onion is perhaps the bulb that many people handle most, and this has relatives in the flower garden. Chives and garlic chives (*Allium tuberosum*) decorate the herb garden, but the taller purple heads of *A. albopilosum* and the yellow *A. moly* are grown as flowering plants, although they sometimes keep an oniony smell.

The flowers of bulbs which grow in early spring seem to have a particular perfection, coming as they do when the winter is hardly over. They include species of *Crocus*, far more delicate than the hybrids; snowdrops; tiny iris, such as *I. reticulata*, *I. histrioides* and yellow *I. danfordiae*; *Anemone blanda*, which is a hardy tuber; and the squills, *Scilla sibirica* which is a brilliant blue and spreads very readily, and the paler *S. tubergeniana*. These are the earliest, most magical flowers, much smaller than the mass of daffodils and tulips to follow, but with a clarity of colour that gives them a special place in the garden. 'February Gold' is a small, early daffodil that naturalizes well and shares the same quality.

Later in the year there are the lilies, some of the most striking garden plants, but they need free-draining soil which should never be allowed to dry out. Raised beds for good drainage, with plenty of humus to retain moisture, will provide the right environment and will repay the effort with fragrance and flowers. Although lilies are particularly demanding, all bulbs do best in well-drained ground and all will rot if they are left in waterlogged soil. Their other main requirement is that their leaves are left for a few weeks after flowering to replenish the food store in the bulb. Trimming the leaves as soon as flowering is over will always lessen flowering and eventually starve the bulb to death.

Herbaceous perennials, which mostly lie dormant through the winter and grow again each spring, include many of our most attractive and well-loved garden plants. Over the centuries they have been grown in many different contexts, but the environment in which they are most remembered, and in which they may be said to look their best, is the herbaceous border. This is a long bed, ideally with some evergreen hedge or a wall as a backcloth. At the rear of the bed are the tallest species, with lower ones in the foreground. In front there is a pathway of grass or some harder material, which allows the visitor to walk along the border, admiring its rainbow of colours. A stroll down a pathway between two well-stocked and maintained herbaceous borders is one of the summer's great pleasures.

The heyday of the herbaceous border

was undoubtedly the final decade of the last century and the years before the First World War. They began as an expression of aversion to the rigours and discipline of carpet bedding and represented a move back to an informal style. They declined as wages went up and the numbers of gardeners employed went down, because a herbaceous border, to look its best, demands long and skilful attention. The mixed borders which replaced them included a proportion of shrubs and were less labour intensive.

It was the size of the great herbaceous borders, many of them almost as wide as a modern plot and stretching far further, that occupied an army of trained gardeners. But on the scale of a modern, small garden, the work involved is not enormous. As the plants grow, they need supporting, so that the taller plants at the back can tower over the border without collapsing into it in the first breeze. As the season progresses, the borders need the usual weeding (not much when densely planted) and dead-heading to extend the season of flowering. Each year, generally in autumn, some plants will need lifting, splitting and replanting so that they can continue at their best for many years.

The greatest disadvantage of a herbaceous border in a modern garden is that it is very seasonal. In the summer it is a delight but in the spring or autumn it can look a little bare. Including in the composition plants which flower early and late in the season can extend the display a little and, indeed, the crisply emerging, perfect new leaves of spring have their own attraction. No matter what you may do, however, it is in the nature of the plants to die back at the end of the year, leaving hardly more than bare earth throughout the winter.

Gertrude Jekyll, who was one of the great artists in the composition of these borders, acknowledged that at different times of the year one walked in different parts of the garden. In a suburban plot you cannot, and each bed must justify its existence throughout the year, hence the prevalance of mixed planting. It would be a pity, however, to lose the summer brilliance of herbaceous planting completely. Its character, and above all its colour, is worth retaining in spite of the labour of nurturing and supporting it, and a certain winter drabness.

There is a popular idea that whereas fabric and paint colours can clash so that they are uncomfortable to look at, flowers cannot. It is as though their natural origins make them in some mysterious way exempt from the rules which govern other pigments. Looking at the random palette of a cottage garden, it is tempting to agree, but cottage flowers, which are closer to wild flowers, are relatively soft in colour. They are therefore easier to mix than modern hybrids which are as bright as any fabric and need handling with almost as much care.

A colour wheel (see page 147) is a circle in which the colours of the spectrum are placed so that each is opposite the colour that complements it. As a tentative rule (sometimes brilliantly contravened), if you divide the wheel in two by a line between red and green, good colour schemes usually come from one side or the other. In practice this means it is best not to mix yellow-reds and blue-reds.

In a long border of 100m (380ft) or so, it is possible to progress through colours in a way that one cannot in small gardens. Gertrude Jekyll's schemes included some that moved from blue and pure yellow, with white, on to a crescendo of hot orange and red colours and then down again into white and pink, lilac and blue. You need the distance to make it work and borders like these can really only be admired and enjoyed but not copied.

Another favourite of hers was the single colour border or bed, which is much more adaptable to a small garden. White borders are perhaps the most popular and there are several famous examples. They use grey and variegated foliage to enhance the flowers. Other colours are possible: yellow works well, again because of the complementary foliage that can be grown.

Foliage is important in the herbaceous border, even though most emphasis is given to the flowers. It can provide a neutral foil between incompatible colours; it is also, of course, the part of a herbaceous perennial that is longest on view, so a plant which has attractive leaves to precede and follow its flowers is doubly valuable. It is the dense mass of foliage that gives the plant its effective height, so a plant with low leaves and brief, tall spires of flowers should remain at the front of the border.

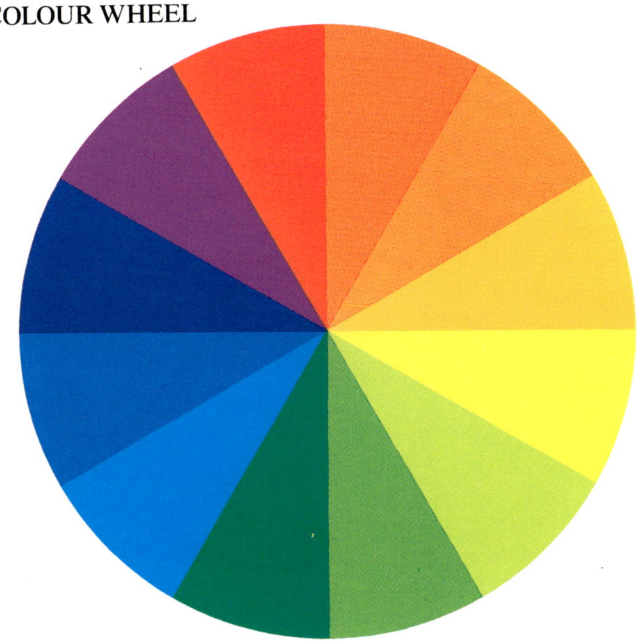

Above left: *White remains the favourite choice for single-colour borders, in part at least because of the wide range of toning grey foliage plants available to complement the flowers.*

Opposite: *Spring bedding with primulas and tulips backed by an unusual wall-trained forsythia.*

Talking about 'rules' for designing the colour scheme of a flower bed is just as hard as it is for a room or a garment or anything else. There are always enough exceptions to make any dogma suspect. Colours are affected by their surroundings, so seeing a plant in one context may not indicate exactly how it will look in your own garden, though it will always be a better guide than the colour printing of a catalogue. Two colours that clash when they are the same tone may not do so if one is much darker than the other. In the case of some bedding, and even more so of containers, window boxes and hanging baskets, the intense vivacity of a mass of clashing colours, brilliant in the sunshine, may be just the effect you need to enliven the garden.

HERBS

The British generally are supposed to be rather bad at using herbs. Certainly it is true that you will see a greater quantity and variety of herbs on sale in any French market than most British cooks will use in a lifetime. But two or three hundred years ago this was not the case; in 1664 the writer and diarist John Evelyn compiled a calendar of some thirty-five species of herbs and salad vegetables, with plants for every season of the year.

Any incentive to experiment with new herbs in the kitchen is probably crushed at birth by the sight of unexciting little jars, apparently containing a grey-green dust, on supermarket shelves. Planting a herb garden may prove to be the secret behind a revival of herbs in cookery.

In planting a herb garden we move, perhaps, closest to the earliest gardeners. The herbs our ancestors knew were planted, as ours are, for their taste and their smell, but mainly to make cures for the sick – the herb garden was both the physician's drug supply and the family medicine chest. The medicinal use of many herbs is commemorated in their binomials; the species name *officinalis* indicates that the plant once had a therapeutic role. Sage, rosemary and borage, which all have this species name, are still consumed, although not often these days with the intention of reducing sweating, aiding digestion or alleviating depression. Other plants which still carry the label *officinalis* and find a place in the garden but no longer in the diet, are more interesting and more surprising; peony and valerian, for example, which can both be very harmful, and *Calendula officinalis* (the common or English marigold) which is no longer in demand as a salve for wounds, but both the leaves and the vivid orange petals can be added to salads.

The making of drugs and potions, which still uses plenty of plant material, has moved out of the home and become big business. Only lavender bags and pot-pourri remain as a reminder of the days when tansy and lavender were strewn round the edges of rooms to deter fleas and lice. By and large, herbs have retreated to the kitchen and even there they have only a shadow of their former status.

Herbs are compatible with any style of garden and the range of possibilities is enormous. They come in a great range of sizes, from ground-hugging creepers, such as pennyroyal and some mints and thyme, to giants of a couple of metres, such as angelica and lovage. They can fit easily into the casual disorder of a cottage or wild garden. The soft grey colours of many of their leaves make them good contenders for a place in a herbaceous or mixed border, where they can separate and enhance more brightly coloured flowers. Many of them do well in containers, so a cluster of pots around the kitchen door can make a very convenient herb bed. Traditionally they were grown in small separated beds or in the formal patterns or 'knots' of the sixteenth and seventeenth centuries. They do seem well suited to this kind of garden and there is practical sense in this arrangement as well, because small beds separated by paths or stones make for easy gardening and also easy harvesting. Presumably the medieval monks who attended to the herbs growing round their monasteries were aware of these benefits when they planned their gardens.

Knot gardens were generally edged with a closely clipped miniature hedge, often dwarf box. Other alternatives today might be well-clipped cotton lavender (*Santolina chamaecyparissus*), which has finely divided silvery leaves, or a low-growing English lavender, such as 'Munstead Dwarf', although this makes rather fat plants for a position of this kind. In a small herb garden it is as well to use one of the herbs themselves for an edging of this kind – chives are ideal for the summer but disappear completely in the winter; hyssop and thyme are evergreen and will

A small collection of herbs perfectly integrated into the garden as a whole.

also make dense enough growth if regularly trimmed.

Another quite common but successful design for a herb bed is derived from a cartwheel; the shape is laid out in stones and the plants are grown between the spokes of the wheel. Yet another would be to base the plan on the shape of the fanlights that crowned so many front doors in the nineteenth century. Or use the sunbursts that decorated doors, windows and gates during the 1920s and 1930s. The herbs can be separated by rows of bricks, by narrow paths, or by areas of different coloured gravel.

Many of the herbs in common use have variegated varieties which can be planted for their contrasting appearance, although on the whole the originals have the most flavour. Clusters of different varieties of the same plant look well together, such as the dark green leaves of peppermint alongside the mid-green of spearmint and the brilliant gold of gingermint. There are several hybrids and varieties of thyme, with green, silver or

gold leaves which can be combined in the same way. Sage has purple and 'Tricolor' forms and fennel can be green or bronze. The mass of delicate dark leaves produced by an established clump of bronze fennel makes a very striking background to other, paler, foliage and flowers.

The position of a herb plot within the garden as a whole is also important. The first consideration is its proximity to the house – it is clearly convenient to keep the ingredients for a recipe as near the kitchen as possible. In addition to this, many herbs smell wonderful when brushed against, walked over or even just shaken by a shower of rain, and this is another reason for keeping them beside a path or somewhere else within the reach of your nose. Creeping thyme, coriander, peppermint and 'eau de Cologne' mint are often planted in this way.

Another important factor when planning the position of a herb bed is the origins of the plants themselves. Many of them were introduced from southern Europe or even farther south, and although they will tolerate some shade, they will always grow best in a sunny position. The problem for most of them seems to be a cold damp soil rather than frost; they will go through a hard winter unscathed providing the drainage is good, but perish if the soil has any tendency to become waterlogged.

A small part of the jardin potager *in the garden of the château at Villandry in France: a beautiful garden on a grand scale using the colour and form of vegetables to great effect.*

VEGETABLE GARDENS

The conventional approach to growing vegetables is to hide them. There is a historical precedent for this – in large gardens, they were grown in walled enclosures along with flowers for picking; something to be used, eaten and enjoyed, but looked at as little as possible. In small gardens today they are usually relegated to the farthest corner and camouflaged by a trellis, whereas in very small gardens they are hardly grown at all. However, a single glance at a vegetable garden such as that beside the Château de Villandry, near Tours in France, must surely convince anybody that it is possible to make a vegetable garden with as strong a claim to beauty as any flower garden. There is also a great deal of pleasure to be had in picking and eating your own produce, in knowing exactly how it has grown and what in the way of fertilizers or pesticides it has absorbed.

The garden at Villandry was redesigned in the early years of this century, and has areas of ornamental garden as well as a lovely *jardin potager*. This is laid out in squares, each containing geometric vegetable beds edged with box, enhanced by standard roses and arboured seats and finally surrounded by trained fruit trees. Each square has beds of different shapes, but all are based on engravings of gardens made in the sixteenth century by Jacques du Cerceau, and all are planted with vegetables chosen for their colour and form as well as for their culinary value.

The elements of this garden at Villandry can be used on a smaller scale to

A painted seat overlooks an attractive small garden composed almost entirely of vegetables.

grow food in a way that justifies the label 'vegetable garden' rather than the more strictly utilitarian 'vegetable plot'. The choice of the plants themselves is much larger than might be immediately obvious; there are, in fact, a number of varieties of 'decorative vegetable', vegetables grown purely for their appearance and effect in bedding schemes: maize, with leaves in a number of different colours, cabbages with frilled and variegated foliage and dark red beet are three of the most common.

On the other hand, there are several plants grown for the kitchen today which began their careers, some centuries ago, in the flower bed. For example, the crimson-blossomed or square-codded pease of the sixteenth century is now grown as the asparagus pea, but its red flowers and four-lobed, frilled pods are as pretty as ever. If you grow it to eat, it is vital to pick the pods when young, or they will become too tough.

Tomatoes are another example. They were introduced from tropical America in the sixteenth century and were believed first to be poisonous and then, under their old name of 'love-apples', an aphrodisiac. They were long grown for their looks rather than their taste. As recently as the mid-nineteenth century, they were described, rather begrudgingly, along with sea food, as 'an acquired taste'; today, their flavour is one of their most important characteristics. Even without the protection of a greenhouse, there are fruit which ripen to every shade of yellow, orange and red and even one or two which are striped, such as the variety 'Tigerella'. Their sizes and shapes vary too, from the tiny, round 'cherry' tomatoes to irregular monsters such as 'Marmande'. One favourite, a tiny 'cherry' tomato with a good flavour, is 'Gardener's Delight'. The fruit is carried on large triangular trusses which, as it ripens, look almost like bunches of red and green grapes. It is a vegetable to admire and not to hide. There is also a range of varieties which grow as bushes and can be cultivated in pots, tubs or even hanging baskets. It is usually almost impossible to find any but the most common varieties of tomato as young plants, but the seeds germinate easily and can be grown on a window sill if necessary.

Runner beans, with their brilliant red flowers, were another introduction from the New World to colonize the flower garden before stepping into the kitchen. There are white-flowered varieties too, and in a decorative garden either can be grown up a wigwam of four or five canes, to form a narrow column, or along a trellis, against a fence or up a wall.

A decorative vegetable garden is also the ideal setting for unusual vegetables. Many of these are actually older varieties which were grown by our ancestors but are neglected today in favour of the uniformity of modern hybrids, which were often developed to suit the needs of commercial farmers rather than gardeners. There are now signs, however, that some of these older varieties, with their unusual colours and shapes, are no longer the prerogative of slightly cranky gardeners, clinging obstinately to their horticultural heritage; instead they are on their way to becoming gourmet high fashion. The colour and taste of many certainly makes them worth trying and a browse through the catalogue of one of the specialist seed companies can be an inspiration.

There are many kinds of lettuce, for example, with heads which are tight or loose and leaves which are frilled or straight and in tones of red and brown as well as every imaginable shade of green. When growing your salad, there are many alternatives to lettuce. Endive (*Cichorium endivia*) is a wonderful ragged plant with a mass of toothed leaves like the wig of a maddened hairdresser; it is pale in the centre and bright green on the outside where the leaves get more sunlight. Endive is no more difficult to grow than lettuce and is a pleasant change to eat. Should it be allowed to go to seed, it repays your neglect with very pretty blue flowers. As with lettuce, there are related species and other varieties in many shapes and colours.

There are also some very attractive members of the spinach family, with dark green leaves contrasting vividly with extra thick midribs of white or red. Known as seakale beet and silver beet, or ruby chard and Swiss chard, all these plants are almost two vegetables in one. The green leaves can be cooked like spinach or eaten in salad, whereas the midribs are of a delicate enough flavour to be cooked separately and eaten like asparagus.

Low-growing vegetables look their best in a dense mass; a bed of carrot leaves, with their lush green fronds, is every bit as pretty as a bed of ferns. There is, however, a deeply ingrained convention that, whereas flowers may be grown in clumps, vegetables are grown in rows. In a large, open piece of ground there is some sense in this, because it enables the gardener to walk in a straight line between the plants and to reach them all. But in a vegetable garden with small beds surrounded by paths, there is no reason not to depart from tradition and grow vegetables in blocks, filling the narrow beds with a uniform mass of foliage. To get this uniform look, space the plants evenly by planting or sowing in diagonal rows and slightly closer together than is generally recommended. The more closely vegetables are planted, the smaller each individual will be, but this loss of size is generally offset by the increased number of plants, so that the overall crop is much the same while the appearance of the garden is greatly improved.

The better and more deeply cultivated the soil, the more closely vegetables can be grown. Deep bedding is a system of cultivation in which compost or rotted manure is spread over the ground annually, but not dug in. This organic material is then incorporated naturally by the endeavours of worms and other organisms in the soil and produces a deep, friable soil with good fertility. As an additional benefit, this kind of bed does not require digging; indeed the whole point is that the soil organisms are left, without the disruption of mechanical cultivation, to do the job on their own.

Over a period of years, the depth of the bed increases and the vegetables can be planted more closely than in ordinary soil. The dense thatch of leaves that this produces not only looks more attractive than a more sparsely planted garden, but it also protects the surface of the soil from the sun, lessening the evaporation of water and reducing the number of visits with the watering can. Deep bedding is ideal for a small garden with narrow beds, because it is very important never to walk on the soil. Once the structure of the soil is broken by trampling, the ground will need digging to let in air. This will disturb the soil organisms and stop them incorporating the humus, thus breaking the natural cycle. Deep bedding is one of those rare occasions when the garden can actually be improved by what looks like a policy of calculated neglect. The technique is often part of an entirely organic regime, when no pesticides or inorganic fertilizers are used at all; as poisonous residues accumulate around the globe, this idea becomes increasingly attractive. However, it is also possible to use deep bedding in conjunction with chemical controls.

LAWNS AND GROUND COVER

The maxim, 'The sight is in no way so pleasantly refreshed as by fine and close grass kept short,' appeared in an encyclopaedia published as early as *c*1260, written by a German, Albertus Magnus. Then there were the flowery meadows depicted so often in medieval manuscripts. Though they might not please the eye of a gardener raised on weed-free turf, they were certainly lawns of a kind, probably based on an idea brought from southern Europe by travelling merchants and pilgrims. By the fourteenth century lawns were also used for playing a number of games, including bowls. Interestingly, the French word *boulingrin*, said to be a corruption of 'bowling green', has nothing to do with the equivalent game of 'boules' which is played on any flat surface, and usually not on grass at all. In French the word *boulingrin* is closer to the old meaning of lawn, an open grassy space.

A small and tranquil lawned garden beside a house in London.

For many people the lawn remains the only proper heart to any garden. Today, some critics regard the small lawn as some kind of cultural hangover from the days of the wide, sweeping, grassy areas of the eighteenth century, and see the suburban lawn as no more than a memorial to the ghost of 'Capability' Brown. In the last decade or so, however, there has been an increase in the use of paving as an alternative to grass in small gardens. There are some obvious advantages: although initially more expensive, a hard surface is cheaper and easier to maintain; paving means the end of tiny purposeless lawns, the end of lawns worn out beyond survival because they cross the most used route to a door, and the end of carrying a lawn mower through a terraced house in order to mow a couple of square metres of grass in the front garden.

A lawn should be laid for a reason, not just because there is a gap in the garden. There are still situations, even in the smallest garden, where a lawn is important and 'refreshes the sight' like nothing else. In a sunny garden it has a feeling of coolness on the hottest day; some plants, particularly foliage plants, are displayed effectively against stone or brick, but many brighter colours are offset better by a surrounding of grass; herbaceous borders cry out for a smooth grassy path between them. Grass also brings a look of the country with it that can be very restful in a suburban garden, and laid in circular or curved shapes it can relieve the inevitable rectangular outline of most of our gardens. On a strictly practical level, a lawn is a softer playground than paving for children, although not necessarily the best surface when bikes are their most important toys.

'Lawn' today means a fairly smooth surface, planted with a mixture of several species of grass, and cut short. Because grasses are fairly hard-wearing they can be walked on, and the way in which they grow makes them particularly suited to repeated cutting and trimming.

The first lawns were made by cutting the grass with a scythe, and beating the turf to flatten it, and you can certainly coerce existing rough turf into a lawn of sorts by much the same methods, but with the benefit of a mower and roller. In practice, however, today's lawns are generally seeded or laid with turf. The cheaper alternative is seed, and this may in the long run also produce a better lawn because you have greater control over the species of grass. But for instant results turf is the answer: it creates a lawn at much the same speed that you can lay a carpet.

Whichever method you choose, the mixture of grasses that you need depends on the use to which the lawn is to be put and the effect that you want to create when it is laid. A 'fine' lawn mixture will produce, potentially at least, a bowling green. But it will not survive the onslaught of dogs and children. For a family lawn that is also a playground you need a coarser or more hard-wearing mixture, with a greater proportion of rye grasses.

Turf is generally sold as consisting of either 'best' grasses or 'hard-wearing' grasses, whereas seed, although it is often bought ready-mixed and categorized in a similar way, can also be more flexible. It can be mixed with a multitude of varieties to suit a site exactly; for example, one which favours the grasses that grow best in shade.

Seed or turf, the basis of preparation is the same for each. Lawn grass is probably the only plant in the garden that has to cope with being cut and trampled regularly, and although we choose grass because it will survive this kind of treatment, it is only fair to give it the best possible start. The underlying soil needs to be well dug, free of perennial weeds, evenly fertilized and level. It is also important to think at this stage about the drainage of the lawn, particularly if you are aiming at an immaculate bowling green, without weeds and free from moss.

The balance between grass and moss in

Mowing more closely in some areas than others gives a variation in texture that is as distinct as a change in planting.

a lawn depends largely on how wet the soil is. Almost any lawn will show some moss after a long period of wet weather, but a badly drained lawn will suffer continuously simply because poorly drained soil suits moss better than it suits lawn grasses. You can rake and poison until Doomsday but it will be a one-sided battle – the moss will always return. The only way to adjust the odds in your favour is to make sure that the land is well drained before the lawn is laid. If the problem is caused by a heavy clay soil then dig in large quantities of compost, peat or other kinds of humus together with coarse sand or grit. In very poor conditions, for example where the water table is high, install a herringbone of land drains which slope slightly towards an existing ditch or drain of some kind or a specially constructed soakaway. It is a major job, but the only way that a fine grass lawn will survive in such difficult circumstances.

Seed should be sown in the spring or early autumn, when the soil is moist and warm, to promote germination. If you sow them in winter the cold may slow germination to the point that the seeds either rot or are eaten by organisms in the soil before the tiny plants emerge, and in summer the soil may dry out completely. Turf is best laid in autumn, unless you are prepared to water conscientiously through the summer. If the turves dry out before they knit together, they will separate so that the lawn looks not grassed but badly tiled.

Once established, a lawn will take as much attention as you are prepared to give it. The man who looks after the municipal bowling green has a full-time job rolling and watering, spiking and feeding. On the other hand, a family lawn of coarse grasses will do perfectly well if mown something like once a week (depending on the weather) through the growing season and given an annual feed in the spring when growth begins. Spiking the lawn, with either the tines of a fork or a special roller, will improve aeration and drainage.

A smooth lawn growing in the sunnier part of the garden while other, shade-tolerant ground cover plants thrive under the trees.

A path made with slabs across grass. Mowing is made easier by setting the slabs slightly lower than the surrounding lawn, as these are here.

The most regular task is always mowing. The longer the grass, the greater the predominance of 'coarse' grasses. In the summer, except in times of drought when both should be left a little longer, a fine lawn should be cut to a little more than a centimetre ($\frac{1}{2}$in), and a hard-wearing lawn to three times that. The grass will grow better if it is cut little and often, and never mown too hard.

A lawn which is carefully mown with a cylinder mower will take on pale and dark stripes, depending on which way the mower has been pushed. These give a very tidy, cared for, rather 'English' look, and an undoubtedly period feel somehow reminiscent of a slower, less complicated world. In small gardens they work best on rectangular lawns and should be mown down the garden rather than across it. They date back to about 1830, when the first mowers were devised. Before that all grass was cut with a scythe, an extremely expert task which, done properly, is still thought by some to have produced the finest, smoothest turf. Rotary mowers, which include those that hover, will not produce stripes but are much easier to use on slopes or where the surface of the ground is irregular.

The easiest lawn to mow is one surrounded by some kind of paving, set slightly lower than the level of the lawn. This enables you to take the mower right over all the grass and avoids the need to trim the edges separately. A line of bricks or paving between lawn and flower bed also allows low-growing herbaceous plants to overflow a little from their bed without taking light from and so damaging the grass. Paving laid like this, however, defines the lawn with a very clear, hard line. Ultimately, ease of maintenance has to be balanced against the appearance you wish to achieve.

If there are trees shading the lawn, the grass beneath them will suffer. The dense summer foliage will block the light and the tree roots will deprive the grass of food and water. It may be necessary to reseed the lawn each year to maintain it, or it might be better to replace it with paving or ground-covering plants which cope better with the conditions.

Access to the lawn is also important. If the only way on to it is through one narrow entry, that area will soon become worn from over-use. A path which leads round the lawn rather than on to it avoids this. If you must regularly cross a lawn then make an effort to vary the route.

The time that a lawn demands depends also on your tolerance of weeds. If you can view a few daisies and a little clover with equanimity, the job will be easier. In a natural environment, leaves rot where they fall and this helps to replace the soil nutrients used by the growing plants. But in a garden the tops of all the plants are clipped and the trimmings are thrown away; this is the exact opposite of what happens in nature and means that the soil below a lawn can easily become deficient in nutrients. On poor soil weeds grow better than grass; to some extent they can be kept down by restoring the nutrient balance of the soil. You can mimic nature by leaving a layer of clippings on top of the grass; this layer will eventually rot into the soil, but it can also form a suffocating mat and cause even greater problems for the grass beneath it. It is better to give the lawn an annual spring feed, using a nitrogen-based fertilizer.

The plants that make successful lawn weeds are those which can live in the same conditions, and can cope with being cut down once a week. Many, such as yarrow, daisies and dandelions, form flat rosettes, which cling to the ground and so escape the mower altogether. For a weed-free lawn, there are selective weedkillers which send broad-leaved plants into a fatal spasm of wild distorted growth but leave all the grasses unharmed. It is worth remembering, however, that there will be fewer weeds in the long run if the ground has been properly prepared before the lawn is laid. Even in 1260, Albertus Magnus pointed out the importance of rooting out all the weeds and then killing any remaining seeds with boiling water before laying turf, which should then be 'beaten down with broad wooden mallets'. The principle remains the same, even though weedkillers make remedial treatment easier.

Lawns which include flowering plants as a virtue rather than as weeds are increasingly popular today, largely as a result of conservation movements. They must surely be the direct descendants of the medieval flowery meadow and have a number of advantages which recommend

A meadow lawn on a moist, acid soil with buttercups predominating.

them to the modern gardener: they are very pretty; they are cut infrequently – indeed in many cases they must not be cut in the early part of the summer or they will not seed and therefore not flower the next year; and they provide food and shelter for wildlife, especially insects, in a way that a conventional lawn cannot. If the length of the grass is an inconvenience in early summer, then mow a path through the meadow rather than cutting all of it. Where the grass is mown, the wild flowers will decline, except for those species which are normally considered as lawn weeds.

A wildflower meadow is best begun from seed. Turning an established lawn into one is almost impossible, because neglecting the grass encourages only a very small number of 'weeds', and does nothing for the wildflowers you wish to establish. It is possible to introduce mature plants one by one with a trowel, or to scrape away some areas of grass with a rake and sow wildflower seeds, but by far the best way is to begin with a flower-grass seed mixture and an empty prepared bed; there are a number of mixtures available, for different soil types and locations. These wild lawns are also a good site in which to establish clusters of 'naturalized' bulbs, such as daffodils, because the growing grass of late spring hides the untidy leaves that follow the bulbs flowering. These leaves make the food that will be stored in the bulb and will fuel the growth of the next year's flowers, so it is important not to cut short this process by damaging them. Daffodil leaves should be left for about six weeks.

A grass lawn is not the only way of creating a soft-textured, open space in a garden; there are a number of other low, creeping plants which can be used, as long as the area will not be subjected to too much wear. Since medieval times there has been a tradition of using camomile for both lawns and turf seats. 'Earth apple', as camomile was once known, from the apple scent of its flowers, was popular in the sixteenth century and has been used on and off ever since. In fact, it makes quite a tough surface, said to grow even more vigorously when trodden on. Wild

Camomile, sometimes also grown as a lawn, here planted in a traditional stone seat.

The thyme lawn at Sissinghurst in Kent.

camomile, *Anthemis nobilis*, has daisy-like flowers, described by a Tudor writer as 'white in the ray but yellow in the centre'. There is also a double variety, with white flowers, as well as 'Treneague' which does not flower at all, and is the one most often used for lawns today.

Other possibilities, again both scented, are pennyroyal and creeping thyme. The species of thyme most often used are varieties of *Thymus drucei* (also called *T. serpyllum*), because these form a flat creeping mat rather than a hummock. There are white- and pink-flowered forms as well as the original purple one and they flower through most of the summer. Given a light trim as the flowers fade in early autumn, they will even flower again and sometimes still show colour into early winter. Pennyroyal is close-creeping and flowers late in the summer.

All three creeping plants spread by growing out from the centre and rooting where their side shoots make contact with the soil, to form new plants which also spread and interlace to cover the ground completely. To lay a lawn, begin with young plants and set them in staggered rows about 15cm (6in) apart for camomile, and 30–40cm (12–15in) apart for thyme and pennyroyal. If they are planted closer together, they will certainly cover the ground more quickly, but as the plants meet they will, in effect, collide and may push each other up into hummocks, spoiling the smooth surface.

One of the problems of using spreading plants to cover the ground is that when they grow outwards, they sometimes leave an empty, dying core. To maintain an evenly covered lawn, you need to root out this dead centre from time to time and then resite some of the newly rooted secondary plants so that they will quickly grow over the gap. Pennyroyal is particularly prone to this.

The only other major problem with non-grass lawns is weeding. Selective weedkillers distinguish between grasses and broad-leaved weeds and kill the weeds, but there is no weedkiller which can distinguish between different species of broad-leaved plants. All the weeding must therefore be done mechanically, that is, by hand or with a hoe, and this means that it is even more than usually vital to rid the plot of weeds before you begin planting.

Other plants, slightly larger but still on the whole low-growing, are often used today as 'ground cover'. This is sometimes no more than a device to save labour, because once the ground is densely covered by the leaves of one plant, weeds will be almost entirely suppressed. It is also useful under trees where there is not enough light or moisture to support grass, on steep banks where mowing grass would be inconvenient or dangerous, and on small areas where the whole business of getting the mower out once a week just for a tiny pocket handkerchief becomes too much of a bother.

The range of plants that can be grown in this way is almost infinite. The easiest are fairly fast-growing, spreading plants, but slow-growing plants will cover in the end and meanwhile the gaps can be filled with annuals. Even plants that do not spread can be used if planted densely enough.

Although the main motivation for planting ground cover is often practical, it can have a unifying effect in a small garden; there is nothing ragged or bitty about a smooth sweep of vegetation round a garden. The best ground cover is evergreen – plants such as *Hypericum calycinum*, which spreads by putting out horizontal stolons just below the soil surface and expands into a dense carpet just as large as it is allowed to become. This plant is extremely common, perhaps the most frequently used ground-cover plant, but only because it is so well suited to the job. It has bright yellow flowers, evergreen leaves, spreads like wildfire and grows anywhere.

The periwinkles are almost as good and will even survive in the dry shade under trees. *Vinca minor* grows only a few centimetres off the ground, whereas the larger *V. major* has shoots which reach about 30cm (1ft) before they arch over and root where the tips touch the ground. There is also a variegated form.

Ivy also does well in dense shade, particularly the variety known as Irish ivy (*Hedera helix* 'Hibernica' or sometimes *H. hibernica*) which has large green leaves. A number of other varieties, with leaves streaked with white or yellow, will grow in a little more sun.

Several species of juniper can be used, including the creeping juniper, *Juniperus horizontalis*. They are not the fastest growing plants, but the wait is worth it. They look wonderful cascading down a sunny bank with their grey foliage, their arched branches echoing the slope of the ground, and they do well in neutral or alkaline soil. On acid soils and in a sunny site, heathers are a natural choice, and there are varieties which flower in every month of the year, although to create a patchwork of colours would spoil the unity achieved by ground cover of a single species.

There are any number of small flowering plants which retain at least some of their foliage in winter and make good ground cover. For example: aubrieta, moss phlox (*Phlox subulata*), perennial species of *Iberis*, London pride, thrift (*Armeria maritima*) or perennial alyssum (*Alyssum saxatile*). For shade, bugle (*Ajuga reptans*) spreads by runners, forming a very dense, low covering with vertical stems of blue flowers in early summer. There are a number of varieties: 'Variegata' has leaves of green and yellow, 'Rainbow' (also called 'Multicolor') is pink-bronze with yellow and 'Atropurpurea' is a strikingly dark purple.

Among the low shrubs, *Gaultheria procumbens* is very attractive, with shiny leaves and white or pale pink flowers followed by red berries. The rock rose, *Helianthemum nummularium*, grows vigorously, especially in a sunny, well drained position. There are many named varieties, with flowers in all shades of red and yellow, through to white. To get a bed of one colour it will be necessary to buy plants of one variety, but if you want a mixture, they are easily and cheaply grown from seed. They flower profusely in June and July and need cutting back quite brutally with a pair of shears once the flowers are over or they will get leggy and lose the dense compact appearance that makes them attractive as ground cover. Pruning in spring removes the young flower buds, even though they are not yet visible, and prevents flowering that year.

As with a lawn, the key to successful planting of ground cover is getting the soil clear of weeds beforehand. The greatest villains are, as usual, the perennial weeds which have persistent and spreading root systems: couch, bindweed, ground elder and the like. If these weeds recur and their roots get entangled with the roots of the ground cover, almost the only solution is to dig the whole lot up and start again. If the ground has harboured these weeds, you can only be sure that they have been completely removed if it is left untouched for some ten summer weeks without any sign of their reappearance. Once the ground cover is established it will repay the effort.

PAVING AND PATHS

Choosing paving is a matter of balancing appearance, practicality and cost. Traditional paving materials, such as brick and stone, are attractive but expensive, whereas modern materials, such as concrete, are cheaper but considered 'nastier'. Both, however, can be used to make a surface which is thoroughly practical and hardwearing. All hard surfaces must be laid on adequate foundations, depending on the wear they receive, and with a slight slope to allow drainage.

If you are using stone, the best way is to follow the lead of geology and use stone that is native and natural to the area. It will be cheaper, easier to get and may well match the material already used for the house. In regions where there seems to be no local rock types, most of the stone used in paving is sedimentary in its origin (either sandstone or limestone), and is cut into slabs by splitting along a natural

Irregular paving made from pieces of broken stone make a sunny informal terrace beside a summer house. Plants growing in the crevices between the stones link the paving to the overflowing pots and beds.

A beautiful brick path, largely in a herringbone pattern and typical of the work of Gertrude Jekyll.

bedding plane. So the rock is, as it were, pulled apart in the same way that it was laid down or deposited. When exposed to the weather and a million passing feet, some erosion or wearing of the rock inevitably occurs and it is this that creates the attractive, evocative surfaces of old stone paving. Newly quarried stone is very costly, but old slabs can sometimes be bought from the local council when pavements are replaced.

Granite paving is more unusual than other kinds of stone. It is not a sedimentary rock and is extremely hard, which is why it is often used to make kerb stones. Granite tends to be found in shades of grey or pink, depending on where it is quarried, and it can be polished. Polished stone is only suited to a very formal design and seems, somehow, to look more at home in sunnier climates. It is also lethally slippery when wet. A better way of using a hard stone like granite in a small garden is as sets. In appearance, these are not unlike grey bricks, but with a slightly curved face. They are usually laid vertically, exposing the small, square end, and they look best in small areas.

It is almost always cheaper to buy broken pieces of stone than cut slabs and, as the gradual cracking and breaking of stones is one of the reasons why old pavements are replaced, stone pieces are often available. These irregular fragments are usually relaid in a random pattern, known appropriately enough as crazy paving. It is hard to believe that broken slabs have not been used for utilitarian paths over many centuries but, in fact, the technique became popular in Europe only in the 1920s. It is a very useful way of paving with stone that you could not otherwise afford, but it needs enormous care if it is not to look muddled, formless and untidy.

Firstly, it is really only suited to an informal setting. Its essential irregularity tends to mean that it neither takes the eye away, down the garden, nor focuses it on a central area of interest. This makes it very hard to use in a strong, clear design. Its random shapes, however, make it easier to use in a curved path than square or rectangular slabs.

Secondly, it is important that the stones are closely and carefully fitted together, so that there are no substantial gaps between them. The only exception to this is in paving that is to be interplanted, when gaps can be left and filled with earth to hold a plant. This can look very effective but is easier to maintain if a number of clear plant spaces are chosen, rather than allowing vegetation to grow round every stone.

Thirdly, a random effect is sometimes spoiled by laying certain combinations of stones, for example if the joints form a continuous line, which can dominate the pattern and draw the eye away from the rest of the garden. All in all, because the exact laying of this style of paving is so important, it is advisable to play around with the arrangement of the stones before fixing them.

The most difficult part of crazy paving is the edge, because small stones tend to crack away from the main area into the flower bed, or whatever lies round it. Small stones are often found round the edges because the paving is begun in the middle, with the biggest and best pieces, and then allowed to deteriorate steadily as it spreads outwards. The solution is to reserve the largest pieces of stone for the outside, and so make it as firm as possible. This can give a clearer, more formal pattern to the paving, which can be emphasized by further breaking up the small slabs in the central part.

Another way of making the most of crazy paving is to arrange it so that it makes clear rectangles which are then themselves put together as though they were whole slabs. It is also a good way of using broken stone alongside whole slabs where you do not have enough for the entire area to be covered.

Brick paving is very popular, particularly in a small garden where the small size of the bricks is compatible with the scale of the surroundings. Like stone, bricks come in many colours and shades and may have a local identity. Like stone too, they are sometimes prohibitively expensive. Old bricks may be cheaper, and also more mellow in appearance, but they may weather badly and fall to pieces if laid as paving. Bricks are made and fired in different ways for different needs so that house bricks, although they will last a hundred years in a wall, will if laid in a path, absorb water and begin to disintegrate in the first frost.

Various brick patterns can be used for paving: there are traditional designs, for example, with evocative names like basket-weave, ladder-weave and herringbone. Herringbone probably requires the most skill in laying, because the bricks have to be cut at the edges. They can be laid either flat or on edge. Laying on edge, that is with the stretcher face upwards, gives a finer texture, but is obviously more extravagant in its use of the material. Some designs incorporate bricks in both attitudes; for example, a line of bricks on edge makes a strong surround to a pattern of bricks laid flat. Brick paviers are a modern innovation, made specifically to avoid the problems of using ordinary bricks in paving. They are thin, brick-sized slabs, which are both frost-proof and hard-wearing.

The variety of cast slabs is enormous

Cobbles can be used to relieve and break up a path made from slabs of either stone or concrete. They also make a surface which is relatively hard to walk over and so slows progress around the garden.

and it is worth getting catalogues from manufacturers rather than relying on the selection available at a garden centre. They are made in many textures – smooth, or rough with exposed aggregate, or riven so that they resemble eroded stone. They can be cast to look like a square of bricks or sets, with a segment of a curve on some slabs to enable a pattern of circles to be laid. They can be large or small, square, rectangular, octagonal, hexagonal or round. They can be cold grey, warm honey, brilliant terracotta and many other colours too. The choice is wide and must depend on both use and appearance. Smooth slabs are best for a terrace where chairs or tables are used, but something rougher and less slippery is better on a path or near water.

In a small garden it is important to use slabs that are on a similar scale and in colour that matches the house. Patterns using several colours may be tempting, but can look brash, particularly when the stones are wet, and all the colours darken markedly. Patterns that use more than one size or shape of slab, or small rectangular slabs laid in one of the traditional brick patterns, can be more effective.

Clearly, as a modern material concrete

A diamond-pattern path that could be made using bricks or granite sets in gravel, between two beds of iris.

needs to be used with great care in any other context. Sadly, it is often in its most boring form – large white slabs, laid corners together with no thought or detail – that it is visualized. Used more carefully, as part of a design, it is as valuable a paving material as any other.

Loose stones of various sorts and sizes can make a good, firm surface. Gravel, for example, has many colours, depending on the rock from which it is derived, and many textures, depending on the size and shape of the particles. Naturally occurring gravel, also called shingle, is worn and rounded by water whereas chippings have sharp edges. Pea-gravel has the size and shape its name suggests, and gives a very uniform surface. Gravel is relatively cheap but it is essential that it is properly laid. To obtain a firm surface it should be rolled on to a material called hoggin, which contains clay and, on top of the usual, essential hardcore, binds the gravel together. It needs a hard, surrounding edge to stop it from spreading into lawns and flower beds. It also needs occasional rolling to keep the surface firm, particularly if it has much rough use. Gravel has to be weeded meticulously or treated annually with a weedkiller.

Uneven stones are generally a slow surface to walk on, which makes a cobbled street an irritation but cobbles in a small garden something that contribute to a leisurely stroll. Cobble-size stones can also be laid in patterns or used with other materials; indeed mixing materials can be the very best way of creating an interesting and detailed texture in paving. A brick outline of squares or diagonals along a gravel path, or random stone slabs surrounded by cobbles, work well. Gertrude Jekyll and Edward Lutyens combined forces to make a number of gardens, and several of these have interesting combinations of brick and stone slabs, with gravel and cobble stones. Mixed paving needs to be planned out before it is laid, so that the balance of materials is right but, done well, it has considerable virtues. It enables you to use contrasts in size, so that the finished effect is neither too bland nor too dense in texture. It allows links of colour with the surrounding architecture, without having a whole area of paving in exactly the same brick as the house, and it is one of the best means of making a well crafted and carefully thought out paving from cheaper materials.

A Victorian bedding pattern adds interest and character to a straight gravel path.

Pebbles that are larger than gravel but smaller than cobbles can be found in every colour imaginable and can be combined to make a complex pattern or even a picture – the kind of pavement that is better called a mosaic. Other materials can be incorporated as well, such as old slates and roof tiles used side up as narrow rectangles, or small units such as half bricks and granite sets. On a large scale, a pebble mosaic would be a herculean task, although they were popular in the seventeenth and eighteenth centuries. They are also often seen in China and in southern Europe, beside villas or round Byzantine churches. The patterns are sometimes geometric, and sometimes simplified pictures of trees or birds, animals or fish. Pebbles of the palest white and densest black make a vivid contrast under the brilliant blue Mediterranean sky. Under greyer, northern skies and using, perhaps, subtler shades, pebbles set in mortar can be used in a similar way. Working on a small area at a time, so that the mortar does not set before the pebbles are in place, the creation of a mosaic can be very satisfying as well as a striking and highly personal feature in the garden.

BOUNDARIES AND DIVIDERS

Hedges, walls and fences, all barriers of some kind, can be used round a garden to contain it, or within it to make a division, to create a perspective or to frame a view. Whatever their function these structures will have a marked effect on the overall style and atmosphere of the garden. The character of the boundary fencing is determined, at least in part, by practical considerations; most gardens need to be surrounded by something, whether for shelter, seclusion, privacy, or just to keep children and animals safely in or firmly out. But this fence is also part of the garden itself. As well as marking the dividing line between the world you have created inside the boundary and the world outside, over which you have no control, it is part of the hardware, like the paths and buildings that frame the garden and complement, or not, the design and plants within.

As well as round the perimeter of the garden, walls and hedges can be used inside it, to make different areas, almost like a series of rooms. They are a way of changing the character of quite a small garden from one area to the next, so that if you yearn for both the classic style of a formal garden and the abundance of a wild one, you can, for once, actually have the best of both worlds. (There is a garden laid out like this on page 54.) Traditionally the part of the garden closest to the house has been the most formal, often turning in on the house and reflecting the architecture in its design.

Between the wars many suburban gardens were split in a similar way, to separate the ornamental garden, close to the house, from the vegetable plot, the orchard or rougher, less cultivated grass beyond. The division was usually marked by a hedge or trellis, with an archway through it – a style that still persists, often very successfully as a way of separating a playground from the garden or of reducing the area of the garden that has to be maintained.

A division which is visually less dense than a fence or wall – a trellis perhaps, a very low hedge, a row of shrubs or a line of pleached trees – can actually make a small garden seem larger. It allows a clear view down the garden, but nevertheless holds the eye at the barrier, so that when you are looking at it the end of the garden is unfocused and recedes into the distance. In some cases a single tree or an island bed in a lawn can create the same effect.

If you erect a fence or wall round your garden, you may need to consider the law of the land and the local planning regulations as well as your own tastes and finances. In a town, many local authorities have limits on the height of fence that can be built without planning permission. A back garden fence is generally allowed to be 2m (6ft 6in) high, but if it borders a road and affects sight lines, then the regulations may change.

It is always politic to discuss your fencing plans with your neighbours, and in some places you are obliged to do so by law. Domestic boundary disputes, whether about the ownership of a fence or the exact position of the line between two properties, are extremely difficult to solve, often because there is no clear evidence to support either case. There may be maps in deeds, but drawn to a scale too small to be useful, or the information in one set may simply contradict the information in another. It can develop into bitterness and acrimony, and can be avoided only by getting the whole thing clarified by a solicitor before you buy the house – which is no help once you have moved in, but worth remembering for the next time.

Hedges

A hedge is a kind of living wall, made from a row of shrubs or trees, pruned so that they stand as one and the individual plants become indistinguishable. Almost any shrub can be used in hedging – evergreen or deciduous, green or flowering, shaggy or immaculate – and the size can be anything from a tiny box edging round a herb knot to a towering screen of conifers. Hedges can vary enormously in character, from the close-clipped, tall, smooth yew, typical of the grand gardens of seventeenth-century France, to the cut and laid hawthorn hedging used to enclose animals, from the small but breathtakingly intricate parterres of Italian and French formal gardens to the colourful informality of a mixed hedge in a cottage garden.

Opposite: *One of the beauties of yew, whether grown as a tree or clipped as a hedge, is the bright colour and texture of the new growth in spring. In this corner both untrimmed and newly cut yew shows this young wood and blends delightfully with the green tones of* Alchemilla mollis.

An archway cut through a dense hornbeam hedge frames the view of spring bedding plants.

Holly, yew, hawthorn, hornbeam and beech are among the most traditional shrubs used for boundary hedging. The first two are evergreen. Hawthorn is deciduous, but the branches grow and interweave so densely that the hedge looks solid even when bare. Its tough thorns make it ideal for enclosing stock, and it was one of the earliest hedges known. Beech and hornbeam are both deciduous, but although their leaves turn russet in winter, they do not actually fall off until the following spring, so the hedge has some colour all winter. Privet (*Ligustrum ovalifolium*) is a relatively recent introduction, brought from Japan in the mid-nineteenth century, and seems these days to be used for suburban hedging above all other plants. It thrives in every location, apparently entirely impervious to urban grime and pollution. *Lonicera nitida* is an even more recent import, brought from China in the early years of this century, and now very popular. It is evergreen, with minute leaves, and is often suggested as a faster-growing alternative to box. But although it makes a very adequate hedge, it lacks the gloss and characteristic charm of box.

Strangely, both *L. nitida* and privet, which are hardly ever seen except as hedges, form rather attractive shrubs when left unpruned. Both have yellow or golden varieties which, when used in a hedge, can look very bright and harsh but seem less so when the shrub takes its natural form. *L. nitida* grows long arching branches and has a very spiky overall shape, whereas privet grows tall but remains fairly dense. Arguably, these reliable but rather boring hedge plants are better left as shrubs.

Over several centuries hedges have played an important part in garden design, as smooth formal hedges or complex and even fantastic pieces of topiary. The smoothest hedges are created with plants with small leaves, hence the use of yew and, for smaller projects, box. Hedges made from larger-leaved shrubs, such as beech, hornbeam and laurel, look tidy enough when clipped, but never have the crisp exactness and precision of line that can be achieved with yew and box, or even with privet or *L. nitida*. Several conifers can be clipped to a smooth finish and will make a good, evergreen tall hedge or screen. The best-known is the Leyland cypress (× *Cupressocyparis leylandii*), which is notorious for the speed of its growth. This has led to its reputation for being unmanageable – certainly, if left to grow, the plants will reach 30m (100ft), but they can be stopped by taking their tops off when they are as tall as you want them, and are not really the horticultural monsters they sometimes seem. *Thuja plicata* (the western red cedar) is another conifer which has rather brighter foliage and is slightly less vigorous in growth than the Leyland cypress, though the final height achieved by the unpruned tree is actually greater.

There is plenty of opportunity for variety in the form of a formal hedge. If one plant every few metres is allowed to grow just a few centimetres wider than the rest, and clipped square, the effect is one of buttressing. This can be a very effective way of breaking up a straight length of hedge, squaring a narrow garden, making divisions for different flower beds or delineating a space for a seat. A slightly lighter effect is achieved with a buttress which is deeper at the base than the rest of the hedge but cut back to the width of the hedge at the top at a steep angle. The top of a hedge need not be horizontal; it can be cut into battlements or regular curves, or allowed to project at intervals and then cut into a shape, making an archway over a path perhaps, or a peak, cone or ball or something more complex.

Topiary was once the name given to the whole art of ornamental gardening and in Roman times a topiarist worked throughout the garden. Since then the meaning has become restricted to the careful pruning and clipping of hedges which creates an assortment of shapes, both simple and bizarre. Topiary has always been popular (except, perhaps, during the eighteenth century when it was to some extent excluded by the landscape gardeners), and can still add shape and character in a modern garden. The simpler forms, like balls, cones and hemispheres, can be used as a major element, rather in the fashion of a Dutch garden, or as part of many other designs. Enthusiasm for topiary was not restricted to the landed gentry but extended to cottage gardeners; there were many informal and utilitarian gardens which

A massive yew hedge grown in giant battlements frames a stately carved stone seat.

Perfectly smooth yew hedging used for ornament, as punctuation in a formal garden rather than as any kind of barrier.

also had a clipped peacock beside the gate. Hedges are usually made from the small-leaved evergreens that are also used for formal hedging. The shapes can be anything from simple but highly decorative spheres and cones, to teddy bears, steam engines and other whims of fantasy. More complex shapes, such as peacocks, need support and should be grown up a shaped frame until the bush reaches the required height, before clipping is begun. It is a slow but fascinating business.

When making a more basic shape, and for most hedges, the general principles of pruning apply. When you cut the leading shoot, you encourage the plant to develop side shoots and bush out. This is exactly right for a hedge, which needs to thicken as soon as possible, or for a low dense shape, such as a hemisphere. It is quite wrong for a tall, narrow cone. For a cone, leave the leading shoot until it has reached the final height before cutting it at all.

The smooth exactness of a formal hedge is part of its character and it must be made and maintained with precision. It is almost impossible to judge any aspect of its shape by eye, so it is better to use tools and guides right from the start. To plant a straight hedge, mark out the line with a pegged string and put a single row of young plants along that line. For a curved hedge, use a hose pipe to indicate the exact planting line. When the hedge is mature, clip the top with reference to a fixed horizontal line, or use a plank and a spirit level. Although a hedge is, in many ways, the living equivalent of a wall, it should not be cut so that the sides are vertical, but so that it is slightly narrower at the top than at the base. This looks better, makes a sturdier and more natural shape and also ensures that the lower branches are not overshadowed and completely deprived of light. The slope of the hedge is called the batter, an eighteenth-century building term which also applied to banks and walls. The angle

Variegated Canary Island ivy grows quickly and soon covers a fence or trellis with dense foliage. Grown on even a wire fence it has the appearance of a hedge.

of the batter can be measured by using a frame with a plumb line to set the vertical and a movable arm to show the line of the hedge. This 'batter rule' is still used to cut large formal hedges. In the hierarchies of the great gardens of the past, maintaining the hedges was regarded as one of the more skilled jobs in the garden, but in the absence of a staff of skilled topiarists, the modern gardener has to work slowly and carefully and learn by trial and error.

A formal hedge made from more than one species of plant is sometimes called a tapestry hedge. The name gives some idea of how delightful it can look when it is well thought out and maintained. The best way to plan one is to choose a plant for the main 'background' and then add small amounts of two or (perhaps in a longer hedge) three other species. Because an occasional, single plant of a different species will either look insignificant or make the hedge look rather spotty, it is better to plant species at least a metre at a time. In the best tapestry hedges the different plants and colours interweave, rather than grow in stripes, so as the plants grow, be prepared to prune them with secateurs to get the best shapes where the two species meet, before cutting the surface with shears in the usual way. Quite subtle combinations of shades of green produced, for example, by some of the hybrids of holly, or the gleam of beech with yew, look wonderful and infinitely more attractive than the very common and overbright combination of golden and green privet.

For a more informal hedge, the choice of plants is very wide and includes deciduous and flowering shrubs, as well as evergreens. One of the virtues of an informal hedge is that it is not so rigorously trimmed that the shrubs are prevented from flowering. Species of *Pyracantha* and *Cotoneaster* are sometimes used to make more formal hedges, but they hardly flower and consequently bear very few of the brilliant berries that make them so attractive in the winter. Several species of *Cotoneaster* are suitable for hedging. A number are evergreen whereas others, such as *C. simonsii*, lose some or all their leaves but keep their berries into the winter, or at least until the birds find them. Pyracantha is a hardy evergreen with a number of species which make good hedges. They have dense clusters of white flowers in the spring followed by red, orange or yellow berries that both brighten the hedge and attract the birds.

Both these genera make their new growth (on which the flowers are borne the following year) after flowering. If the new growth is shortened in September, as the wood ripens, the hedge will be kept fairly tidy, and there will be enough wood left to flower and carry berries the following year. Any more major pruning, to alter size and shape, can be carried out in the spring, before the new growth begins, but will restrict flowering for that season. As always, any dead, damaged or very spindly growths should be cut out whenever they occur.

Two other evergreens that make lovely hedge plants are *Escallonia* (for example *E. macrantha*) and some species of *Pittosporum*. They are both able to withstand salt breezes and make wonderful seaside hedges and windbreaks, but neither are very hardy in cold winters or

The rose 'Penelope' used as a hedge.

on poorly drained soil. In a warm garden they are both very attractive – escallonia has red-pink flowers, while *Pittosporum tenuifolium*, which will grow to as much as 4.5m (15ft), has pale green leaves with wavy edges (often seen in florists' arrangements). Left on the plant, they provide an interesting texture.

Several species of *Berberis* are also used to make thorny and impenetrable hedges, and have been recommended for that purpose since the sixteenth century. *B. darwinii* and *B.* × *stenophylla* are both suitable but, although they have bright flowers and berries, they tend to make a hedge that will grow to be rather wide for a small garden.

An informal hedge can be made from a complete mixture of shrubs, though again it is better not to plant different species singly, but to use at least two or three together. A mixed hedge like this can be delightful, with all kinds of colours and scents to enjoy, and also offers the opportunity to add perennial and annual climbers, such as clematis or *Tropaeolum speciosum* (flame creeper), or *T. canariensis* (canary creeper), as well as shrubs such as shrub roses, *Forsythia* spp., tamarisk, the snowberry (*Symphoricarpos* × *doorenbosii* 'White Hedge'), various rhododendrons (where the soil is suitable), *Mahonia* spp. and a host of others. However, a mixed hedge demands mixed care: each different shrub needs pruning in a way that will suit its particular mode of growth and flowering, so you cannot cut the whole hedge at the same time. From the point of view of maintenance, it must really be regarded as a row of separate shrubs.

Three, wild, deciduous plants which are also included in many nurserymen's catalogues – hawthorn, elder and spindle tree – will make a mixed hedge of rural character. The common hawthorn (properly called *Crataegus monogyna*) has been used to make hedges for as long as people have grown plants to keep their animals close to home. There are several closely related species and a number of hybrids, which generally have brighter flowers as well as bigger and better berries, but *C. monogyna* is the most robust and the one most often used in hedging. Common elder is *Sambucus nigra*, and there are yellow-leaved and variegated varieties available; the spindle tree, *Euonymus europaeus*, also has a number of cultivated varieties. There are a number of evergreen species of *Euonymus*, some with variegated leaves, and these are commonly grown in gardens, often against a fence or wall, but the flowers and fruits are much less conspicuous than those of the wild, deciduous tree. Spindle 'berries' are pink, heart-shaped fruits which open to reveal brilliant orange seeds and are produced in the greatest quantity when there are several trees about to allow for cross-pollination. The brightness of their colour undoubtedly makes them attractive to children, but they are poisonous.

One of the problems of deciding to surround your garden with a hedge is that, however carefully it is fed and nurtured, it will not be useful as a barrier for several years. If it is important to enclose the garden meanwhile, erect a temporary fence of some kind, which will be replaced by the hedge as soon as it is mature enough. Wire netting is often used as a temporary fence, but a better choice is some kind of solid screening, such as a wattle fence or hessian or plastic of some kind stretched between posts, because this will also act as a windbreak, protecting the young plants and giving them the fastest possible start in life. Sheltering plants can be as effective a way of promoting growth as raising the temperature. In most small gardens the biggest danger is that surrounding fences or buildings are so arranged that they form a wind tunnel which causes plants to suffer from sudden and vicious draughts – these damage them more than the exposure of wide open spaces.

A mature hedge is such a large and established feature in the garden that it is easy to forget that it makes the same demands on the soil as any other collection of plants. Once established, the hedge will have a wide-reaching root system which may deprive nearby plants. As with any permanent planting, the ground should be thoroughly prepared with compost and bonemeal before the young plants are put in. Continue to feed with a general-purpose fertilizer each spring and water well in dry weather, for the sake of both the hedge and its neighbours.

Walls

Walls of brick or stone are today a very costly choice because both the materials and the skilled labour needed for their construction are so expensive. The choice of materials available is enormous. Stone can be very beautiful, particularly when it is of local origin and matches the house, but is probably the most expensive option of all. Reconstituted stone blocks, made from crushed stone, are made in regular shapes and consequently are easier to transport and lay than the natural rocks from which they come. There is also a variety of concrete building blocks, some moulded to look like stone, which can be used successfully.

Concrete has a rather unsavoury reputation – it is believed automatically to be modern and ugly. In fact, it was used by the Romans, has a long and very respectable history as a versatile building material and can be of enormous use in garden construction, whether as purchased blocks or cast *in situ*. Concrete blocks are made in a range of colours and textures and can also be cast mixed with a lightweight aggregate which makes them particularly suitable for a situation like a roof garden, where weight is a problem. They can, in addition, be painted easily after construction. Concrete is best regarded as a material in its own right and not chosen only when it is disguised as stone or some other different material.

A brick wall, with its fine texture, is very often most compatible with a small garden. Brick houses built before the First World War were generally constructed with bricks made locally, because transporting such a heavy material was so difficult. Now there are far fewer brick fields, so finding bricks to match your house may not just be a matter of using the same local materials. But there are still literally hundreds of different colours and types of brick available and if the walling material is well chosen to complement the building material of the house, it will draw the house and garden together. If

A serpentine or crinkle-crankle wall warming and supporting tender fruit trees trained against it.

you can afford it, a brick wall does have a number of other advantages. It is one of the very best background surfaces on which to display plants. In addition, many plants actually grow better against it, because during the day it absorbs heat from the sun, and after sunset it loses it slowly, thereby extending the day of the plants growing against it, and working, really, just like a storage heater. This is the reason why the more tender fruit trees are so much more successful against a brick wall than when free-standing.

Garden walls need adequate foundations. They also need to be wide enough to support their height, to have buttresses at intervals, or to be staggered in some way to provide extra stability. All in all, building a wall is, perhaps, an occasion for expert advice. From the eighteenth century, serpentine walls were built with curving lines to make them stable without extra thickness and buttresses; they were used to support fruit trees. The origin of these walls probably lies in the fact that they saved on materials and were consequently lower in cost, but their horticultural value was soon recognized and, whenever possible, they were built running from east to west so that fruit trees planted in the bays would benefit from sunlight falling on them from every side.

The arrangement or pattern of bricks within a wall is called the bond. To some extent, the bond affects the strength of the wall, but it is largely a matter of appearance. There are a number of standard bonds, but old walls often show rather different patterns which give the surface of the wall a more interesting texture. For a greater feeling of unity, the bond can also be repeated in the pattern of paving close to the wall.

Many gardens have a wall of some kind facing into them either as part of the house itself or as a boundary with a neighbouring building. If this catches the sun, it is well worth exploiting it and growing fan or espalier fruit trees or tender shrubs against it. The L-shape of many Victorian and Edwardian houses, made by building a back kitchen extension across half the house, also creates a walled corner, a sheltered space enclosed on three sides by the house and its neighbour. Depending on the aspect, this corner will be a suntrap, which can be made brilliant in summer with annuals and pelargoniums, or a gloomy alley, abandoned to the dustbins. Raised beds built to create a change of level against the wall, or some shade-tolerant shrubs, such as *Choisya ternata*, can transform it. If you grow any kind of plants against the wall of the house, it is very important to ensure that the soil does not rise over or bridge the damp course.

Fencing

Before redesigning a garden or planting new plants, the condition of any existing fencing should be examined with some care. On the one hand, any kind of fence is expensive and it would be foolish to replace it unnecessarily. But if it is already deteriorating, it will probably time its final collapse to coincide with the maturity of your carefully chosen climbers, and the loss of the fence may well also cause the demise of the plants that clothe it.

For reasons of economy, or because it is essential to have instant privacy, many people put up a wooden fence round their gardens. For the same reasons, most of these fences are made from kits of one kind or another, which can be bought from garden centres, DIY chains or by mail order from specialist dealers. Most of these will have already been impreg-

A woven fence, framed with white-painted timber and hung on posts with decorative finials, is entirely changed in character. Compare this with a similar fence, but unadorned, on page 151.

nated with a non-toxic preservative, and this is very important; if you paint a fence with a creosote preservative, the vapours will kill or damage any plants they reach and nothing will grow on it for at least a year.

Wooden fencing which is visually solid and will provide seclusion of some kind, is generally sold in panels of a couple of metres in length, and in a range of heights. There are a number of styles, notably close-boarded (vertically or horizontally), larchlap and interwoven fencing. An entirely solid fence, such as close-boarding, gives maximum privacy but can look very hard and dense. It increases the tubelike feeling of a narrow garden. A slightly open fence, such as an interwoven fence, one that is close-boarded with the planks on alternate sides, or a trellis with a covering of plants, can often provide a less dense barrier which is nevertheless enough of a visual interruption to create a feeling of seclusion. It is also worth remembering that the height of a barrier needed to make invisible a seated or prone figure in the garden next door is much less than that when the figure is standing; a good compromise may be to have a lower fence or wall topped by an open trellis.

There are also a number of less solid fences, including trellis panels, picket fencing and the low, horizontal boarding often called ranch fencing. All fence panels hang between vertical posts which are structurally the most important part. The strongest posts are concrete, set into a submerged concrete block. Wooden posts are best bolted to a concrete or metal 'foot' which is set into concrete. Wooden posts set directly into the ground will rot, even if treated, and will also rock in the wind. Setting the posts themselves into concrete will prolong their life, but the wood will still eventually rot. As so often seems to be the case, the slowest, most complicated and costly way of putting up a fence will last longest and, probably will be worth it in the long run.

The most vulnerable part of a post, particularly if it is made of softwood, is the open endgrain. Underground, this can be kept as dry as possible, and protected to some extent, by placing it on a flat stone. The top of the post is best

A trellis archway leading on to a lawn bounded by a herbaceous border. Behind the border is a low wall with a similar trellis, carrying climbers, built over it.

capped with an impervious material, such as metal, or with another piece of timber cut so that the long grain is exposed. Because the first part of any fence to rot will be where it touches the soil, it should either be positioned above soil level or put on a gravel board which can be replaced when it rots, without disturbing the rest of the fence.

Trellis fencing must have a firm supporting surround. The concertina-type trellis, which is the cheapest, is relatively flimsy under any circumstances, but adequate when firmly pinned between slats. Simply opened out and nailed to the top of a fence it is a short-lived disaster. One of the instantly recognizable characteristics of old trellis work, and indeed of old walls, fences and other garden structures, is the care and craftsmanship that went into their construction, something which is often, regrettably, absent from modern structures. A trellis was made to fit its position, with curves and shapes to enhance its function, not simply attached to the wall in whatever basic shape the manufacturer found easiest to produce. Today's commercially available materials are used to best effect when they are adapted to fit an individual design.

If you inherit or erect a standard wooden fence which looks rather ugly, it can be covered quite quickly with climbers and shrubs. This can be a very effective way of making something that looks quite like a mixed hedge but is much narrower, because the shrubs are tied in to the fence, and therefore more suitable for a small garden. (Suggestions for shrubs which are suitable for hedging can be found on pages 168 and 171.)

A fence which is visually more interesting can often be made by combining different materials; for example, a low wall with higher brick pillars which support shallow wooden fencing panels; or picket fencing, which is quite attractive but low and open and therefore not useful as a screen, can be set above a low brick wall to make a higher barrier. The effect can be enhanced by using tall wooden posts, perhaps with an ornamental cap, and fixing the fencing so that the top of it makes a series of uniform curves rather than a straight line.

The same low picket fencing can be ideal for a front garden, and again, its overall character and appearance can be greatly altered by very minor changes to the materials themselves. Although traditionally a rural material with a rough finish, picket fencing can be made to look more urban with smooth sanding; painting or staining it, particularly in a dark colour, increases the effect. Painted white, it looks very smart in either a rural or urban context, but also needs an annual coat of paint if it is to stay that way. The shape of the tops of the slats also alters the overall impression of the fence: they can be cut into peaks, rounded, cut straight across (although only if painted because this most exposes the end grain) or diagonally. The slats can be mounted so that the top of the fence is exactly horizontal, or undulates in a series of upward or downward curves. Spacing the slats widely makes the fencing look more informal and looks good with a hedge growing above it.

An alternative to the standard fencing of the DIY store is to make or commission a construction of your own design. The

Classic seventeenth-century French treillage, *designed by Le Nôtre for a garden in Paris.*

most suitable site for a fence like this is often the front garden, where the need for a boundary is more psychological than real, and a high, close-boarded fence looks dark and secretive. You can use a real fence for inspiration, or a pattern from some other source, or pure imagination. The trellis on page 66 is a case in point; it is derived from a late nineteenth-century window frame which in turn was probably copied from a design of the eighteenth century. The results are best if the pattern is of a size which will repeat several times across the garden, and can perhaps also be used in a gate.

A fence in the front garden is often more decorative than practical, although if it protects your garden from the attentions of passing dogs it will be serving a good purpose. It has, nevertheless, always been important to have some kind of wall between the house and the road. The symbolic importance of such barriers is shown by their nature over the years; the arrow-headed iron railings of town houses, like the miniature battlement walls of mid-twentieth century suburbia, emphasize that, however modest, home can indeed be a castle.

STRUCTURES AND DECORATIVE FEATURES

Trellises

The excavation of Pompeii, the patient removal of the countless small pieces of pumice that smothered the ancient city when Vesuvius eruped in 79BC, revealed many details of Roman city life and horticulture. Among the relics are frescos, or wall paintings, which depict massed flowering shrubs and trees, statues and fountains, all viewed through a lattice fence or trellis.

Trellis-work has survived from then until the present day, in large and small forms. On the one hand it can be used to support climbers and enliven a tiny courtyard, while on the other it was one of the specialities of the Le Nôtre family, master gardeners for three generations in the extravagant grandeur of seventeenth-century France. The french word *treillage* remains in English to describe trellis that is used in a suitably grand manner.

A trellis can be attached to a wall or left free-standing. It can be erected to support climbing plants or used, primarily, for its own effect and, in either case, it can to some extent deceive the eye. As a fence, it allows a restricted view of the garden beyond. It has been used as a way of camouflaging a vegetable garden without shortening the view, which a solid fence would have done by making it disappear altogether. Used with shrubs and trees beyond, it can give the impression of greater space than actually exists, in just the same way as the frescos of Pompeii.

Fixed to the wall, a trellis can be used in a variety of *trompe l'oeil* effects which give the impression of three dimensions where there is only a blind wall. A common style in the past contained an arch which appeared to lead into a tunnel or bower of *treillage*, with its perspective receding into the distance – this charming effect was produced merely by arranging slats on a flat surface. A small arched bower can also be made, or at least an impression of it created, by curving the vertical struts to a central peak and bending the horizontals to mimic the lines seen in perspective. It works well at a distance, but in a small garden would clearly be a curiosity rather than an effective piece of fraud.

Historically, most trellis-work has been made of wood – willow, hazel or Spanish

Painted trellis can be used to make pillars and other structures that will support climbing plants, often roses.

chestnut – which presumably was grown, coppiced and split in much the same way that it is today for the manufacture of the far more utilitarian chestnut fencing. Iron was used for some supports in the enterprises of the seventeenth century, and much more in Victorian times when intricate metal and wirework was also fashionable for arbours and garden furniture. Rustic trellis, with the bark left on the wood, was popular around the turn of the century, when there was a swing towards a less formal style of gardening. Today, most of the prefabricated commercial trellis is made of cedar and is often already either painted or treated with a preservative.

Ready-made trellis, whether for a plant support or as a feature, can be used quite simply. If it is to be free-standing, either alone or perhaps to raise the height of a boundary fence, it is important that it is firmly fixed to a series of uprights and that the trellis is enclosed by a frame. If it is used without this kind of support it will fall down or be warped and finally pulled apart by the twining stems of climbers. The best way to make the frame for a trellis is to enclose it between two strips of wood with a thin fillet, and then to cover the frame and end grain with a final strip. This looks very tidy and well finished and is as weatherproof as possible.

If a trellis is to be fixed to a wall, then it

This trompe l'oeil *trellis works perfectly; the illusion of depth is so strong that it is hard to believe that the structure is actually completely flat. It is an unusual example of the technique in that it is so small and simple in design.*

should be held 2.5cm (1in) away from the wall so that the stems of the plants climbing up can grow right around it. This can be done using purpose-made fastenings or short lengths of old piping or cotton reels. The weight that is carried by trellis is greater than it looks; all those delicate winding stems add up to a substantial burden, so it is important to secure the structure with wall plugs.

If you have an essential but unattractive building in the garden, such as a garage or shed, it can be transformed by covering it with trellis and then climbing plants. Some wall shrubs will have the same effect, but more slowly, and will also need attaching to the trellis if they are to reach a useful height.

A number of other structures can be made with trellis, such as an arbour over a seat. There is a very simple example in the garden on page 90, or something rather more romantic could be made by imitating one of the arbours in the *potager* at Villandry and covering it with jasmine, honeysuckle or a scented climbing rose.

Arches and pillars, like those in the garden on page 54, for example, are also successfully made using trellis-work. It makes a substantial-looking structure much more easily and cheaply than brick or stone and also gives proper support for plants climbing up it. The roses that climb trellises are not truly climbers – they just have backward-pointing thorns that tend to lodge wherever they touch and prevent the plant falling back, so on any kind of trellis they are best tied in from time to time.

Pergolas

Pergolas, which can also be made using trellis, have a history just as long. The word comes to us from the Italian, but there is evidence that they were built in ancient Egypt and in Pompeii. They abound in every classical and medieval source. Like so many features of garden design, they probably began as something entirely functional, as support for a vine, or a way of making a shady path in a hot climate, for example. Once established,

Above right: *A nineteenth-century pergola at Bodnant in Wales.*

Below right: *A hole in a wall turns a moderately pleasant view beyond into a perfect picture.*

they became highly regarded for their ornamental value, and in Renaissance Italy they were built with decorative stone pillars and lighter wood or iron arches. Since then, they have been made from stone and brick, from metal and every kind of wood. They have been festooned with plants for food, flowers for scent and constructed in every position the garden has to offer, from round the perimeter to straight down the middle.

In a small garden today, pergolas still offer a number of possibilities. In the past they have generally been associated with a path or walkway of some kind, but they are now also built close to a house, as a unifying feature between house and garden, and function rather like a verandah. In this context, they sometimes resemble, superficially at least, the pergolas designed early this century by Edwin Lutyens, with architectural pillars in materials to match the house, and heavy wooden horizontals overhead. Whereas Lutyens worked in English oak, today's pergolas are more likely to be made from softwood with a coat of preservative. If the supporting pillars are too light and look as though they lack substance and proportion, they can usually be widened at the base by planting an evergreen shrub round the bottom. Once a framework of horizontal pieces is in position, other, lighter struts can be put in to help the climbers across the gaps.

Metal arches can be bought and linked together to make a pergola of variable length (there is an arched alley like this in the cottage garden on page 30, grown over in this case with cordon fruit trees). The same sort of thing is also made in plastic. This kind of archway can be an ideal method of progression from one section of a garden to another and can carry a variety of plants, for food or for decoration. Two of the most popular must be species of *Laburnum* and *Wistaria*, both of which have profusely flowering, pendulous blossom, and are breathtakingly dramatic when in flower.

Longer, arched walkways really work best in a small garden if they are against a building or a boundary fence; in a central position they are over-dominant or out of proportion. They can be used as a shady way around the garden, in the medieval manner and covered with a range of coloured and scented climbers, or as somewhere to sit and admire the rest of your labours.

Garden architecture

Most garden buildings are a complete reverse of the general rule that garden features begin as a matter of practical convenience and then pass on into the world of ornament and design. Temples, pavilions, obelisks and rotundas, structures with no real use at all, were admired and copied from Italian gardens of the sixteenth and seventeenth centuries. They became an integral part of the first landscape gardens, often part of a bizarre selection of Gothic follies and classical ruins, alongside, perhaps, a hermitage and its resident, salaried hermit. In the nineteenth century there was a brief fashion for garden cottages built in a variety of, supposedly, national styles. There were designs from Scotland and several countries in mainland Europe, as well as from Russia and the Far East, including the 'Bengal cottage' with mud walls and bamboo window frames.

Today, buildings in small gardens tend to be more utilitarian and prosaic – a summer house or potting shed maybe but not, generally, a temple or rotunda. Some period reproductions are worth considering, although many need quite a large

Cordon fruit trees, laburnum or climbers such as wistaria and jasmine can all be grown to cover an arched pergola reminiscent of the walkways around some sixteenth-century formal gardens.

A garden pavilion with some detail and period character that is also unpretentious enough to include in a modern garden.

space and a background of trees or tall shrubs to give them surroundings of sufficient dignity, and all are expensive. Victorian arbours, made in wirework and often painted green or another dark colour, echoed the circular shape and open walls of the rotunda. They were full of twirls and curlicues, which were characteristic of the craftsmanship and passion for detail of their age, and are often omitted from modern reproductions. Photographed for catalogues, they often look rather stark and even slightly comic, almost impossible to imagine in a real garden, but set into a green lawn and festooned with old-fashioned roses they convey a strong period feel and an attractive air of light romance.

WATER

Pools and ponds, lakes, cascades, waterfalls and fountains; from the extravagant grandeur of the fountains of Italy to the studied tranquillity of a mountain lake in Japan or the calm of a trout pond in a medieval monastery, at every time and in every place water has played an important role in the making of a garden. In a small garden today, however, it is easy to feel that, for the first time in history, circumstances have left us with no room for water, that limitations of space have forced out the lakes and fountains of our ancestors, leaving nothing in their wake. It is, of course, not true; lakes may have become pools, but a small amount of water, arranged carefully, can still have a surprisingly large impact.

A pool can evoke in a garden an atmosphere of calm and peace. It can, with a waterfall or fountain, provide life and movement or even a touch of humour. It can be a focus of interest by holding fish or attracting wildlife. It gives another dimension to the range of available plants or a clear reflecting surface to mirror the passing clouds or enhance the impact of its surroundings.

Even a pool created by removing a couple of paving slabs or made from half a wooden barrel can add something to a garden that is, in size, hardly more than a courtyard.

Give the pond a clear, simple outline. Intricate shapes and narrow peninsulas may seem fascinating as an idea but they will look fussy when finally realized in the garden. There are some exceptions, but it is generally true that in a small garden formal shapes are most successful, whereas informal shapes need more space to work effectively. A pool also needs to be integrated with the rest of the garden design and not just dropped into the lawn as an afterthought. The planting around it, the materials of the surround and the shape of the pool itself should all link with the rest of the garden.

Water need not be still and calm. Moving water is always lovely, both for its soft babbling sound and for its appearance, particularly when sunshine brings it, glittering, into life. Now it can be achieved with an ease that would have seemed miraculous to our forefathers. Where 'Capability' Brown might have ordered the diversion of a river to feed water through the garden, technology now provides the electric pump. It really is a minor revolution for the small gardener, to be able to install a fountain or waterfall without cisterns, tanks or hydraulic pumps and to send a fountain leaping into life with the flick of a switch.

The installation of the electricity to power these devices in the garden is best tackled with the help of an expert. Water and electricity are a very dangerous

A modern garden with a raised terrace bridging the pool and overlooking the fountain.

combination. The protection of cables across the garden and the connection of those cables to the mains system of the house must be done properly, so that they are weatherproof and do not become a hazard. Incidentally, while having a source of electricity installed in a garden, for the purpose of moving water, it is worth thinking also about other requirements which could be served at the same time, such as lighting or a point for powering electric tools, so as to avoid the use of a long extension cable.

Enormously complicated, electric-powered, multi-jet fountain systems are available to rival the grandeurs of Rome, but most are entirely out of place in a small garden. A simple fountain looks best, and the pump to power it can often be submerged in the water beside it. The pool and fountain are part of a closed system with the pump circulating the water round it. This means that the level of the water may need topping up in persistent dry weather. The height of the fountain should not be greater than its distance from the edge of the pond or the wind will blow water out, again causing the level to fall. Generally speaking, the pump will not withstand freezing temperatures and will need to be removed from the water for winter storage.

Water pouring from one level to another may be less dramatic than a fountain, but can be used very effectively and again can be powered by a pump, either in the water or in a box close by. A trickle of water from a narrow lip is often as effective as a torrent, and a Niagara-like cascade can be moved only by an enormously powerful pump. There are commercial waterfall pools, made from

A weathered and mossy tank with a small waterspout into a lily pond, further enhanced by careful planting around the edge of the pool.

A seventeenth-century gardening manual demonstrates fountains that are simple, complex and even vulgar.

preformed plastic and complete with changes of level and plastic rocks, but it is generally better to construct your own, using natural materials. The levels of a waterfall can be made from rocks, from slates or slabs, or by making a narrow lip, like that of a jug, from one small pool into a lower one. Cascades of water have often been used in conjunction with a flight of steps, even as a moving handrail. On a small scale, a narrow canal running alongside a path, in the traditional Islamic manner, can be given movement by a small fall that matches the drop of a step. Although there are few occasions when our climate demands such a device to cool the air, it remains an attractive and refreshing feature in the garden.

The best place to construct a pond is somewhere that gets plenty of light, but not direct sunlight all day which may overheat the water, particularly in a small or shallow pond. On the other hand, if a pool is under deciduous trees, it will fill with leaves in the autumn which will poison the water as they decay. In a garden with many trees it may be best to stretch netting over the pond each year to catch the leaves as they fall.

Whatever the size or style of pool, and whether the water is still or moving, the first essential is that the container should be watertight. In the past the most usual way of sealing the bottom of a pond was by using puddled clay. Today there are a number of easier alternatives. One is concrete, which is used successfully for intricate waterfalls or very large designs, but is generally giving way in the small garden to the various kinds of synthetic liners, which are cheaper, easier for the amateur to install and generally very satisfactory. The principle of these is that you dig the hole for your pond, level the bottom soil, remove any stones and make the surface absolutely smooth with a layer of newspaper. You then lay a sheet of the lining material over the hole, anchoring it loosely on the sides with weights, and begin to fill the pool. As the water pours in, it will mould the liner to the shape of the hole. This is probably the simplest method of pond-making yet devised and is extremely successful for formal and informal shapes when used carefully.

There are a number of materials available as liners, and the most expensive is almost certainly the longest lasting. Butyl is said to last as long as fifty years. The size of the sheet you will need can be calculated like this:

> Maximum length of pond + twice the maximum depth + $\frac{1}{2}$m (20in) × maximum width of pond + twice the maximum depth + $\frac{1}{2}$m (20in).

The half metre extra on each dimension gives enough liner to anchor firmly and cover the edges. This can be done using paving stones, bricks or about a hand's depth of soil topped with turf. To make a boggy margin for plants, run the liner under about 30cm (12in) of soil before bringing it up to the surface and anchoring and protecting it in the usual way. It is important to cover the edges completely, partly for appearance, but mainly to protect the liner from sunlight.

Cut logs used to edge a pond and a raised bed in a garden planted with some cultivated varieties and other wild plants that will feed and encourage birds and animals. Behind the pond, the grass is left long to allow the growth of cowslips.

Many garden centres stock pool shapes made from moulded fibre glass, often in an impossible shade of swimming-pool blue. For a very small, symmetrical shape they can be useful, providing you can find the size and shape you want in a dark colour with a ledge for marginal plants, and can avoid fibre-glass rock edgings and so on. They are installed by digging a hole a little larger than the shape, with a perfectly level bottom so that the mould can sit in it squarely. Then backfill with sand or fine soil.

For most of us, a pond without plants would be incomplete and there are many from which to choose. The gardens on pages 42, 54 and 66 contain some of them with suggestions for their use in different locations.

The important thing about plants in water is that they need to grow at a particular depth; they will not thrive unless this is adhered to with some accuracy. Some plants, called marginals or marginal aquatics, need to grow in shallow water so, to accommodate these, the pond should have a shelf round its perimeter at a depth of 20–25cm (9in). These plants include species of iris, different kinds of rush and a multitude of others. Plants that prefer deeper water, including waterlilies, are called floating aquatics. Both kinds actually need to be rooted in soil, even though they are under water, and in a small pond the best way to manage this is by containing them in special plastic baskets. These are filled with soil and planted, much like ordinary pots, and then submerged in the water and supported at the proper depth.

Water plants, particularly submerged aquatics like waterlilies, easily grow too large and will fill a small pond. They can be controlled to some extent by being planted in baskets, but the real key to the matter is to choose a species or variety which suits the size of pond. Some waterlilies, for example the hybrids of *Nymphaea* × *marliacea*, are beautiful, reliable and easy to cultivate, but just too vigorous for a pond that is small or shallow. A pond that is choked with leaves will give no reflecting surface and will inevitably look undersized. There are plenty of species, however, that are more restrained in growth, and some miniature varieties, such as *N. pygmaea*, which would suit the tiniest pool.

A fish's eye view of the snails and oxygenating plants that play a vital role in maintaining the life and health of every pond.

Perhaps the most important role played by plants in a pool is maintaining the oxygen balance. Like all plants, aquatics use carbon dioxide and water in light to photosynthesize and make food. The oxygen that is a by-product of this process is vital for the other organisms in the water, and without it very little but algae will survive. The species that are the most productive and efficient oxygenators are known as submerged aquatics, a name which is slightly misleading because some of them flower above water in the summer. All areas of water need to be properly oxygenated or they will fast become choked with green algae and strands of blanket weed. The plants that give off oxygen include Canadian pondweed (*Elodea canadensis*), water crowfoot (*Ranunculus aquatilis*) and, perhaps prettiest of all, the water violet (*Hottonia palustris*). Because most new ponds go through a phase of being green as the oxygen balance is established and stabilizes, do not be tempted to empty it and start again. Make sure there are plenty of oxygenating plants and wait for nature to sort it out for you.

Fish are a popular addition to garden pools, and the various kinds of goldfish are the most usual choice. Leave the pond to settle for a few weeks before introducing them, then choose the liveliest-looking specimens from a reputable source. They can usually be carried home in a polythene bag, partially filled with water, but if there is much temperature difference between the water in the bag and that of the pool, tipping them straight in may cause a fatal shock. Suspend the bag in the water for an hour or so while the temperatures equalize before you release them. If your pond is tiny it may freeze completely in winter and this will kill the fish, which should therefore be moved elsewhere for the winter. Otherwise they are surprisingly hardy and will survive most winter weather by lowering their metabolic rate and remaining at the bottom of the water. If the pond does freeze completely, melt an air hole in the ice by standing a pan of hot water on the surface.

When considering the subject of animals and ponds, hedgehogs do not instantly come to mind, but if your pool has straight or nearly straight sides, and particularly if it is edged with overhanging slabs, you may, quite inadvertently, be creating a death trap for any of the animals that almost certainly use the garden. They swim well enough, but eventually drown if they cannot climb out. An unobtrusive length of wire netting, partly submerged, will enable any that fall in to climb out and live to spend another night eating slugs and other garden pests.

Currently, there is a movement which encourages the construction of a garden as a small private nature reserve as well as a place to use, enjoy and cultivate. In this context, a pond is one of the most productive and useful features – not a formal pond with goldfish, which will often eat tadpoles and other 'wild' larvae, but an informal pond with boggy edges planted with native marginals, such as watermint and marsh marigolds, that will allow animals and birds easy access for feeding and bathing.

Whether wildlife gardening is to be a short-lived craze or the major contribution made by our century to the history and evolution of garden design remains to be seen. The fact is, however, that as the amount of undeveloped land available decreases, it is inevitable that the land we use for gardens will become increasingly important for wildlife.

BIBLIOGRAPHY

Books in the first section are reference books; of plants, horticultural methods and techniques, and suppliers of garden materials. Those in the second section are of more general interest.

Brickell, C. (Ed.) *The Royal Horticultural Society's Encyclopaedia of Practical Gardening* (Mitchell Beazley, 1979; *Concise Encyclopaedia*, 1983)
Brickell, C. (Ed.) *The Royal Horticultural Society Encyclopaedia of Plants and Flowers* (Dorling Kindersley, 1988)
Ferguson, N. *Right Plant, Right Place* (Pan Books, 1986)
Jellicoe, S. and G., Goode, P. and Lancaster, M. *The Oxford Companion to Gardens* (Oxford University Press, 1986)
Johnson, L. *The Gardener's Directory* (Michael Joseph, 1984)
Reader's Digest Encyclopaedia of Garden Plants and Flowers (1985)

Berrall, J. S. *The Garden* (Penguin Books, 1978)
Brookes, J. *Room Outside* (Thames and Hudson, 1969)
Brookes, J. *The Garden Book* (Dorling Kindersley, 1984)
Bryan, F. *A Garden for Children* (Michael Joseph, 1986)
Carter, T. *The Victorian Garden* (Bell and Hyman, 1984)
Hellyer, A. *Lawn Care* (Hamlyn, 1986)
Jekyll, G. *Home and Garden* (Longmans Green and Co., 1900)
Jekyll, G. *On Gardening* (Studio Vista, 1966)
Jekyll, G. *A Gardener's Testament* (Antique Collector's Club, 1982)
Johnson, H. *The Principles of Gardening* (Mitchell Beazley, 1979)
Page, R. *The Education of a Gardener* (Collins, 1962)
Rorsach, K. *The Early Georgian Landscape Garden* (Yale Center for British Art, 1983)
Scott-James, A. *Sissinghurst* (Michael Joseph, 1974)
Scott-James, A. *The Cottage Garden* (Allen Lane, 1981)
Thacker, C. *The History of Gardens* (Croom Helm, 1979)
Thomas, G. S. *Gardens of the National Trust* (Weidenfeld and Nicolson, 1979)
Thomas, G. S. *The Art of Planting* (Dent, 1984)

Illustration acknowledgements

Bibliothèque Nationale, Paris 172; The Bridgeman Art Library 10, 16; British Library 95; Eric Crichton Photos 41; ET Archive 14/15, 100/101, 138; The Garden Picture Library 18 (Steven Wooster), 19 (Ron Sutherland), 76, 108/109 (Ron Sutherland), 157 (Ron Sutherland), 158 (Henk Dijkman); The Garden Picture Library/Lamontagne 26, 35, 36/37, 44 (top), 63, 71, 73, 87, 88, 114/115, 118, 119, 139, 147, 151, 156, 167, 180, 186/187; J. M. Gibson/Country Life 94; J. Glover 7, 64, 102/103, 122/123, 134/135, 155, 171; Jerry Harpur 2 (Mirabel Osler), 22 (Chris Grey-Wilson), 39 (Thomasina Tarling), 50/51, 65, 114, 131, 154, 164 (York Gate); Michael Holford 12, 13, 105 (Janet Chapman), 106/107 (Janet Chapman), 146; Tony Mott 58, 150; The National Trust (Nigel Forster) 143; Nicolas Sapieha 14; Edwin Smith 32, 96/97, 153; Harry Smith 23, 27, 34, 38, 45, 46/47, 48/49, 50, 58/59, 61, 62, 68/69, 70, 72, 74/75, 80, 82, 82/83, 84, 85, 86, 89, 93, 104, 113, 117, 120 (bottom), 122, 126/127, 129, 130, 132/133, 137, 142, 148/149, 159, 161, 162, 163, 168, 169, 170, 172, 174, 175, 176, 179, 182, 183, 184; Trustees of the Duke of Devonshire, Chatsworth Collection 56/57; Victoria and Albert Museum 44 (bottom), 52, 185.

The publishers would also like to thank Rodney Ingram for original watercolour paintings on the following pages: 3, 6, 9, 11, 17, 29, 30, 31, 33 (top and bottom), 40, 42, 43, 54, 55, 56, 60, 66, 67, 78, 79, 81, 90, 91, 98, 99, 109, 110, 111, 112, 116, 120 (top), 121, 128, 132, 165, 178, 180 (bottom), 181, 188.

INDEX

Figures in *italics* refer to illustrations